JOIN US FOR WEDNESDAY MORNING PRAYER!

We open our barn, the Iron Bell, every Wednesday morning from 7:00 a.m. - 11:00 a.m for people to have their own personal devotional time with the Lord.

There is live worship and it's simply a time to soak in God's presence.
Some people stay for 5 minutes on their way to work, while others stay for several hours.

Would you like to rec̲e̲i̲v̲e̲ ̲p̲e̲r̲sonal prayer?

During Wednesday Morning Prayer
we offer individual prayer appointments
for those who would like to receive personal ministry.

Sign up at the link below:

signupgenius.com/go/wednesday274

PRAISE FOR *JUNKYARD WISDOM*

Roy Goble is a friend of mine. In fact, he's the first friend I ever had. We met just out of kindergarten. He was a guy who was always getting into mischief and I was drawn to him like a magnet. You will be too. It's a holy mischief Roy's been up to since then. Roy's success in the world hasn't led him to the wealthy; it's brought him to the poor and hurting. This beautifully written book is the story of what Roy has learned along the way about love and compassion and Jesus.

— BOB GOFF
CHIEF BALLOON INFLATOR
LOVE DOES + RESTORE INTERNATIONAL

To truly help vulnerable people around the globe, we've got to be smarter and do better. Real philanthropy doesn't start with a check, but a challenge: are you willing to help another person? Roy Goble has accepted that challenge, and he inspires his readers to do the same.

— JACQUELLINE FULLER
PRESIDENT
GOOGLE.ORG AND GOOGLE FOUNDATION
FORMER DEPUTY DIRECTOR OF GLOBAL HEALTH,
BILL & MELINDA GATES FOUNDATION

Roy Goble is a successful entrepreneur with a grand plan. In my circles—Silicon Valley startups and brand evangelism—that's not unusual. What is unusual is that Roy's weapon of choice is hope. Read this book if you want to learn another way to change the world.

— **GUY KAWASAKI**
CHIEF EVANGELIST OF CANVA AND
AUTHOR OF *THE ART OF THE START 2.0*

God calls us all to not conform to the patterns of this world. But non-conformity doesn't mean uniformity. That's why I like Roy Goble and his book. I doubt Roy's going to move into a row house in North Philly with us—though if you want to Roy, give me a buzz!—but Roy's working out his salvation with fear and trembling just like the rest of us. At the end of the day, I'm not interested in people being more like me, but more like Jesus.

— **SHANE CLAIBORNE**
BESTSELLING AUTHOR AND ACTIVIST

Finally! Now there is a way for wealthy Christians to participate in the vital work of reconciliation beyond guilt or shame! In this ground-breaking book, Roy Goble addresses the "elephant in the room" and offers a better way forward through mutual and life-giving relationships with the poor. This book is a win-win for everybody and it's long overdue. I highly recommend it!

— **REV. DR. BRENDA SALTER MCNEIL**
AUTHOR OF *A CREDIBLE WITNESS AND
ROADMAP TO RECONCILIATION*

Roy's clear and passionate voice comes through the pages in a most genuine and challenging way as he peels back the protective coats surrounding his own vulnerabilities. His openness to describing his own personal flaws allows readers to consider more fully the planks in our own eyes. The result is creating an environment of true and honest self-reflection. The text is written in Roy's easy to read down-home style, but make no mistake: the stories will leave you with big ideas to ponder and hopefully pursue.

— MARK ZORADI
PAST PRESIDENT OF WALT
DISNEY MOTION PICTURES GROUP

Roy's insights always capture my attention because he's one of the most widely-read, widely-traveled, and widely-liked people I know. Like Roy, I've been all over the globe, and I've noticed that people who don't want to be preached at still want to be prayed for. God shows up in our lives when we pray—and it's through our prayers that God calls us to show up for others, on His behalf. I love how Buechner puts it: Go where your best prayers take you. That's what Roy has done, from his own community all the way to Central America and Southeast Asia. Where might this book take you?

— PETE GREIG
CO-FOUNDER, 24-7 PRAYER
INTERNATIONAL VICE PRESIDENT, TEARFUND

Roy Goble could easily be sipping wine and enjoying the good life. In some ways he does. But not at the expense of wisely stewarding the opportunities he's been given. I research and write about global issues and cultural intelligence. Roy lives it—and that comes through in the pages of the book he's written. Funny, challenging, and grace-filled are just a few words that describe what's here. Enjoy and be inspired. That's what happened to me from reading it!

— DAVID LIVERMORE, PHD
AUTHOR OF *SERVING WITH EYES WIDE OPEN* **AND** *LEADING WITH CULTURAL INTELLIGENCE*

Roy Goble is witty, smart, and lives life full throttle. His business success gives voice to his work ethic and capabilities. His life success, however, speaks to the wrestlings of a man of faith trying to invest his talents while also bearing responsibility for his neighbor. For anyone who has felt the discomfort that often comes with privilege, this dynamic and engaging book will be an encouraging guide on how to find your greatest life in giving it away.

— KEN WYTSMA
FOUNDER OF THE JUSTICE CONFERENCE
AUTHOR OF *PURSUING JUSTICE* AND
CREATE VS. COPY

Powerful and compelling. Roy Goble masterfully crafts a provocative and beautifully written read while giving us challenging new ideas and food for personal thought and reflection. As a follower of Jesus, he describes conflicts inherent with wealth and poses important questions. Immensely practical and immediately helpful, I highly recommend this book. You will find Mr. Goble to be a masterful storyteller and deep thinker.

— DR. EDWARD BIRCH
CHAIRMAN OF THE BOARD,
SANTA BARBARA BANK & TRUST

Roy Goble is a wrestler: of habits over mere ideas, of actions over mere words, of reality over mere perception. God holds all dimensions of human life in his heart and wrestles on our behalf, so that all may have life—and we wrestle with God in order to find the life we have been called to, and to share it in ordinary, daily terms with our neighbors.

— MARK LABBERTON
PRESIDENT, FULLER THEOLOGICAL
SEMINARY

Roy's book points out that the 'skill of wealth creation has no correlation with the skill in the godly use of wealth.' By sharing his own story, Roy helps us all wrestle with the tension between what we do on a daily basis in our jobs and businesses and how we as Christians address the needs of the poor—those next door and around the world. He encourages us to think about a 'kingdom economy' that focuses on the return when we invest in people's lives and their futures. Throughout the book, we are challenged to wrestle with how we use each day to make a difference.

— MARY ANDRINGA
CHAIR OF THE BOARD,
VERMEER CORPORATION

* * *

junkyard wisdom

resisting the whisper of wealth in a world of broken parts

By
ROY GOBLE

with D.R. Jacobsen

DeepRiver
BOOKS

Jason —
Thanks for all
you do!

TABLE OF CONTENTS

DEDICATION

To D'Aun. I'm so glad I married you.

FOREWORD

Roy Goble is a troublemaker.

If you know him you already know that. But there's a good chance you don't know him, and that's why I'm glad I get the chance to introduce you. Like I say, maybe the first thing you should know about him is that he's a troublemaker.

Partly that's just his natural wiring. I didn't know him in school, but I'm pretty sure he wasn't the kid who got asked by the teacher to be hall monitor. I think he's the kid the hall monitor was mostly supposed to monitor.

But troublemaking isn't altogether bad. The prophets were mostly troublemakers. So were Martin Luther King Jr., Nelson Mandela, and the suffragettes. It depends on what kind of trouble you're making.

It is true that Jesus once prayed, "Let not your hearts be troubled." But that was just once, and it was when his friends' hearts were being troubled by the wrong thing.

I have a feeling sometimes Jesus might say: "Let your heart *be* troubled":

- if you see one of the billions of people who live on two dollars a day or less
- if you see a child growing up without hope of an education
- if you see the victim of human trafficking
- if you see a neighborhood where crime or gangs or drugs are more prominent than games and safety and really good doughnuts
- if you see apathy in your own heart.

Sometimes it's good for our hearts to be troubled. Sometimes we need a troublemaker—and so do the people around us who are in trouble.

You should be forewarned that this book is trouble in more ways than one. Roy is an edgy fellow, and his words tend to be as raw as the contents of the junkyard that is his milieu and favored metaphor for this book. Junkyards tend to have a certain aroma to them, and so do the places in this world most pockmarked with poverty and violence and death. So do Roy's words. If you don't like junkyards, you might not want to turn the page. But then again, if you don't like junkyards, you're living on the wrong planet. And if you don't have room for discards, you'll have a hard time finding any people to hang out with.

More trouble.

So often, Roy reminds us, trouble is what we want to avoid. We try to keep it at a distance. We write a check. We sponsor a child. We take a trip. We read an article. Often we don't even manage to do those things.

But there is a better way.

The better way is to be part of a movement that began a few thousand years ago when some poor, itinerant, homeless, carpenter-teacher got executed and tore down a dividing wall. It's the wall that divides rich and poor, white and black, male and female, slave and free.

It's a wall of Self.

And it comes down in relationship. Relationship with that homeless carpenter and relationship with the countless billions of under-resourced people in whom, somehow, he still lurks.

The idea of relationship that Roy talks about is not giving people a handout or advice or some of our precious wisdom. It's a relationship built on the realization that my brokenness is as profound as anyone's, that my affluence may blind me to my entitlement, that I have as much to learn as anyone.

I can meet anybody on the ground of my brokenness.

Including the poor.

And there, together, we meet Jesus, at the foot of whose cross all needy people meet: rich needy people and poor needy people.

That's the trouble Roy wants to make for you in this book.

And until we meet the ultimate, cosmic Troublemaker, Roy and his book will have to do for a starter kit.

John Ortberg
Menlo Park, California

~1~

JUNKYARD DAYS

"Wake up, Roy."

I opened one eye. The angle of the sun through my window blinds told me it was morning. Barely.

"We leave for the shop in thirty minutes."

The shop, as my family liked to call the place, was a junkyard. Or an "automotive dismantling center" to the people in the industry. A large metal building squatting in a gravel yard. Outside, automotive fluids and cleaning solvents pooled and festered. Each piece of machinery was slathered with oil, from the hydraulic car crusher all the way down to the handheld acetylene torches. The rusting vehicle hulks were grimed and flaking, and anything that wasn't smeared black was dusty and dull. Inside, the concrete floors were covered in a layer of grease, which I was occasionally tasked with scraping. Our unwashed hands made for smudged doorknobs, opaque windows, filthy countertops, nearly unreadable ledgers and receipt books, and an illuminated Coke machine that struggled to shine through the stains. Even the cobwebs were coated in a mixture of oil and secondhand smoke.

It was going to be a scorcher, with the highs hitting triple digits. Dad always wanted an early start on days like that—not that it made a difference. No matter how hot it was, we'd work until the customers dried up around 5 PM. Early starts just meant longer days.

I was twelve or thirteen. Old enough, according to my father, to handle a forty-hour workweek.

He was right, at least physically. But emotionally I hated every-thing about those endless days of lifting and grease and heat. I rolled out of bed with a mumbled curse or three.

"See all the transmissions on the north wall?" Without waiting for my answer, he continued. "I want them moved to the south wall today." Really? *Really?!*

In my brief life as a full-time worker I'd already slogged through what seemed like an unlimited number of junkyard days. But I'd never been given a job assignment that felt so ... heavy.

Each transmission weighed at least a hundred pounds. They were stacked ten feet high on racks built of 2x4 lumber. Dad expected me to climb a ladder, heft a transmission, climb down, move the trans-mission to the other side of the building, carry it up another ladder, and place it on the new rack.

I started right away because I knew better than to complain.

A couple hours later, with me covered in transmission fluid and sweat, Dad realized I needed help. He assigned one of our yard guys to work with me. Jose, in his early twenties, was strong, diligent, and often drugged out of his mind on the latest cheap pharmaceuticals. I liked him.

When we broke for lunch, Jose asked how I was doing.

"Oh, okay," I shrugged. "Just so damn hot. Wish I had more energy."

"Here," he said, and he held out a few pills in his hand. "Try these. They'll give you a boost."

I waved him off—*thanks-but-no-thanks*—and continued my sandwich.

Another guy from the yard joined us. He was recently hired, about Jose's age, just out of jail, and talked a mile a minute. Before long there was a fight brewing over something stupid, but what else was new? I'd heard it all before, so I focused on my sandwich.

The insults got more and more personal, which didn't concern me until the new guy turned to me and asked, "You had sex with Jose's girlfriend yet? Everybody else has."

Just another lunch break at the junkyard.

Jose and I went back to work. We pushed, pulled, and lifted those damn transmissions all day in the sweltering metal shop. I was covered head to toe in transmission fluid, grease, oil, dirt, and sweat. My hands were so slippery I dropped one on my foot—I didn't break anything, but it hurt like hell. And I gashed my forearm open on an exposed nail. But we managed to move every transmission.

At last Dad closed up the shop, and we drove home in silence. No doubt he was adding up the day's profits in his head and making plans for tomorrow. I was struggling to stay awake.

Mom shrieked when she saw me. I must've looked like I'd crawled through an oil pipeline. With a mother's attention to detail, she pointed out I'd gotten dirt and grease in my hair, ears, even up my nose. "And your clothes!" she muttered. "All ruined ... what were you thinking wearing school clothes to work?"

Too tired to respond, I pulled off my shoes, left them on the front porch, and trudged upstairs. I thought about what a lousy day it had been. Up early, a filthy job in crazy heat, a sore foot, a gash in my forearm, and surrounded the whole time by misfits and drug addicts—only to be nagged by my mom as soon as I got home. And for what? To move some stupid transmissions fifty feet.

Dad poked his head through my doorway. I stared at him.

He smiled at me. "Tough day, huh? Makes college look pretty good, doesn't it? A nice job in an air-conditioned office ... sounds good, doesn't it?"

You have no idea, I thought. *You have no idea.*

And *I* had no idea how right he was—and how strategic. He knew exactly what he was doing that day. He wasn't just encouraging me to leave the junkyard. He was forcing me to think about how to create a better future.

A World Away

Todi, a medieval town in Umbria, Italy.

I stood on the terrace of Le Mandorelle beside my wife, D'Aun. We were two days into our time at the cozy bed-and-breakfast. Set

3

on a small farm, the main house was built of local stone, roofed with red tiles, and surrounded by vineyards and views of the rolling hills. Past the vineyards, olive orchards stretched to the horizon. I looked at D'Aun, who produces award-winning olive oil back home in the Bay Area, and I smiled as I thought about how much she was enjoying this.

For the first time in my almost thirty-year career I was taking a break from my business. A *real* break. Not just a vacation with my wife and two kids during which I still checked in with work every day. This was a complete separation. An entire month with no email, no voicemail, and no snail mail.

The respite felt deserved. My team at Goble Properties had my mobile number on speed dial, and normally they had permission to use it any time I was away from the office. On previous vacations I'd taken strategy calls on the trail in Yosemite and read overnighted reports on the beach in Maui. Even Jaguar Creek, the conservation center we ran in the rainforest of Belize, had Internet access, and our staff there had the same understanding: email Roy any time you need his input.

But not this time. It had taken an entire year of planning, but I'd completely disengaged from work.

I'd spent part of the first week at home as an unpaid but enthusiastic intern in D'Aun's olive grove. My twin goals were to avoid getting in her way and, more importantly, to not harm any of her trees. I succeeded in the latter at least. Watching my high-energy wife nurture her trees was incredible, and the traditional "chop wood, carry water" decompression was exactly what my body and mind needed.

I followed that with a few days in Tahoe, California, with my Bible, my writing notebooks, and my hiking boots—though my notebooks got a better workout than my boots.

At the start of the second week, D'Aun and I had boarded a plane bound for Rome, Italy, and two whole weeks of great food, rich wine, and *la dolce vita*. Seeing the ancient city was amazing, thanks to our tour guide, Angelo, who was worth his weight in gold (which felt like what he charged).

But it was the countryside that transported me to another state of mind. Rolling green hills, silvery olive trees lining each road and footpath, and vineyards like a patchwork of promise as far as the eye could see. Pausing in whatever town or village caught our attention, we discovered ancient stone archways, hidden staircases, and forgotten fountains bubbling in courtyards—hidden shrines honoring those who had gone before us. We used our hands to tear open loaves of hot, crusty bread. We hunted down and drank unique local wines.

All leading to Le Mandorelle. We'd arrived on the first day of olive harvest. Joining in the work, we harvested olives from the trees, moved and measured the large containers, and carried the fruit to the mill for processing. D'Aun and I were amazed by the warm *olio nuovo* as it poured into the *fusti*.

During the days, we explored the countryside by car or relaxed at our bed-and-breakfast. We ate dinner in Todi at a tiny restaurant that served the finest *tartufo tagliatelle* we'd ever tasted. Another night we helped our host, Janina, in the farm kitchen, while her friend roasted chestnuts over an open fire. We sampled dozens of fine Italian wines but kept returning to our hosts' 2007 Sangiovese, grown and aged only a stone's throw distant.

We were, in a word, feasting. And we savored every moment.

Distant Storm

The close of another perfect day in Umbria.

D'Aun's phone chimed. It was a text from our daughter, Rachel. Her dear friend Paige had been admitted to the hospital with a mystery illness. She'd recently returned to the States after spending time with Rachel's anti-trafficiking nonprofit in Thailand, so perhaps she'd picked up a travel bug of some kind. But she was young and fit and back home with her family and doctors.

The text was followed by a call from a friend. He asked us to pray for his elderly father, whose health had just taken a turn for the worse.

That was followed by a call from another friend. He was worried about his wife's severe abdominal pains. She was six months pregnant with twins.

And then came news of a tropical storm spinning across the Caribbean Sea, approaching Jaguar Creek. PathLight, our education and development initiative in Belize, was hosting a dozen people.

But that was the least worrying news. There was always a storm approaching.

The next day, however, updates from the other side of the world stalked us across Umbria. Even as we toured the countryside, we could hear the footsteps of our friends' pain and worry from a world away.

It was only when we returned to our room that we discovered everything had come crashing down.

The tropical storm was now a Category 2 hurricane and would pass almost directly over Jaguar Creek. Damage would be extensive.

One friend texted: they'd had a miscarriage.

The other friend texted: his father had passed.

And Paige—in her midtwenties, healthy, virtually vibrating with love for life—was gone, cut down by a rare, inoperable tumor in her adrenal gland.

What was there to do? D'Aun wept. I paced. We googled cancer rates and tracked Hurricane Richard and composed notes of sympathy. There was no question of processing or understanding what had happened. It made no sense, and we couldn't change it anyway.

It hit me: no matter how far I removed myself, or how content I was in my circumstances, the pain of people across the world could reach me. The personal peace I'd so carefully cultivated had crumbled. My friends and family, in their distress, needed me, and I wanted to end our feast in order to sit with them in their fasting.

Facing the Walls

It wasn't wrong to try to take a break from work and stress, of course. But that break highlighted something crucial.

It wasn't merely an Oprah-esque realization about my "connection" to people back home, though that was real. What it highlighted was that *I'd intentionally built walls between myself and other people.*

We wealthy people—and that includes most of you who are reading this book—are adept at putting up walls to insulate ourselves. Walls of comfort, pride, or denial. Walls made of nothing sturdier than distraction, distance, and new experiences.

But those walls don't simply separate us from the pain of life.

Whether we know it or not, those walls separate us from *people*.

And what's most troubling about those walls is that, in the absence of tragedy, such walls *work*.

The more isolated I am, the more likely it is that I won't even know when tragedy strikes. That evening in Todi, when the bad news came crashing down around us, it was all news we couldn't avoid. It came through friends, through family, and through our business. It was impossible to insulate ourselves from it and from the people whose lives had been changed.

But that begs the obvious question: because of my walls, whose suffering *don't* I know about?

* * *

Primarily, our walls separate the wealthy from the poor. These walls between us—sometimes literal walls—matter a great deal.

The wealthiest humans can live entirely surrounded by people similar to themselves. We can fly around the planet on a whim. We find ways to mitigate pain and hardship. We can buy our way out of certain challenges and find countless diversions to occupy our time and attention. We try, many of us, to prove John Donne wrong when he writes, "No man is an island."

By any definition I am wealthy. And if you are reading this for enjoyment, or if you had to choose which items of clothing to wear today, you are wealthy as well.[1]

Just like the rich, the poor are driven to cope with the pain and hardships of life, but they are forced to do so in different ways. The options of the wealthy are unavailable to them. They may never leave the village of their birth or rarely leave the urban neighborhood where they were born. They are, by necessity, more connected to more people, though rarely to the wealthy.

All humans are natural-born objectifiers. The wealthy objectify the poor, and the poor objectify right back.

Jesus, though, never looked at a person and saw a label or an object. He always saw a particular *life*. If we want to follow Jesus, and live like Jesus lived, we need to start seeing other people as Jesus sees them.

The reality is that it can be profoundly difficult for the wealthy to truly follow Jesus. That is a hard truth, but a truth nonetheless.

We wealthy can live as if we simply don't need Jesus. We can buy products and services and experiences that would seem like miracles to the poor. We have access to those who influence the world. And we get caught up in the trappings and temptations of wealth. If we are wealthy, Jesus can be pushed to the margins of our lives—along with those who don't share our lifestyle.

But Jesus, although marginalized in countless ways during his time on earth, *is not content to be marginalized by you and me.*

Rather, Jesus wants to be at the center of our lives, just as he wants the radius of our lives to continue expanding.

---

[1] According to www.globalrichlist.com, if you made $32,000 last year, you are in the top 1 percent of the world's richest people. If you made $100,000 last year, *you are in the top 0.08 percent of the world's richest people.* Even someone working part-time and making less than $10,000 a year is in the top fifth of the world's richest people. And this is considering only income, and not other elements of wealth such as education, place of birth, race, gender, and so on.

Jesus was an expert at smashing through walls. He broke nearly every social and religious and economic barrier of his day. We sense that we ought to do the same, yet all too often we send proxies through the walls. We send prayers and good intentions and annual checks. But those things are not *us*. They can't form relationships. Only *people*, not generous donations, can receive text messages about miscarriages or missed rent.

The kingdom is built on relationships. There is nothing we can send beyond our walls that is better than ourselves. And when we go ourselves, Jesus goes with us.

The surprise I have been discovering, through sorrow and through joy, is that God is calling me to break down the walls I have created between myself and the poor, *because there is something on the other side that I need to see.*

Back to the Junkyard

I am old enough now to reflect on a good chunk of my life.

If not for my father, Ernie, perhaps I would not have become so financially and professionally successful at such a young age. He asked me to join him in running Goble Properties just as our hometown was becoming what we all know now as Silicon Valley. It was a wild ride as we developed properties, some of which he had owned for decades, into industrial parks to meet the growing demand for space.

Yet I think Dad provided me something even more valuable: the experience of growing up in a junkyard.

When my father came home from World War II, he needed to find work. So with a used pickup, an eye for a deal, and a sense of purpose, he created a job. He was a one-man mobile parts distributor, picking up throwaway tires from service stations and reselling them. Tires led to scrap, scrap led to parts, and parts led to whole vehicles—and by the time I was born in '58, Dad owned land for a wrecking yard. In the following years he purchased several others.

At least that's what *we* called them. To everyone else they were junkyards.

I grew up in the main yard, Valley Auto Wreckers, the largest and best-known wrecking yard in San Jose.[2] Surrounded by razor wire and patrolled by the ubiquitous junkyard dogs, the junkyard was like a second home to me. From the ungodly rainbow of wrecked and rusting vehicles in the yard to the rotating cast of characters who worked there, everything was dirty and rough.

Days were filled with copious smoking, casual (though discreet) drug use, spectacular profanity, and occasional bouts of screaming. When a fifty-dollar part could "fall" into your pocket, distrust was rampant, and it extended to the trade in homemade whiskey, illegal fireworks, and smuggled cigars. (I won't even mention the stars of our softball team, One-Ear Joe and Mad Dog.)

At the tender age of five, my job was to walk along a sixty-foot rack of old tires, read the size off the wall of the tire, and write it on the tread with a yellow ink tube.

By the time I was seven, I was sorting hubcaps and finding sets to mount on the wall. Next came heavier parts, like those dreaded transmissions. At thirteen I was driving the forklift, shuttling flattened cars between the crusher and the flatbed that would haul them away. At fourteen, my dad had me fire the yard foreman.

I wasn't doing any of these jobs *well*, mind you, but I was put in positions of responsibility at a very young age. And people were generally patient with my mistakes—undoubtedly in part because my dad was the boss.

My father's unsavory junkyard and its ragtag crew of workers formed me, sometimes in profound ways. Each time a wall breaks in my life, and I am blessed by relationships that cut across privilege and power, I wonder if the seed of that relationship was planted in the junkyard. Perhaps grace was able to grow in the gravel and dirt.

If not for being raised in the junkyard, I might never have raised a daughter who fights to keep Thai girls from becoming sex slaves, or a

---

[2] According to Walter Isaacson, Steve Jobs likely shopped there when he was a kid.

son who has traveled to three continents creating films about the plight of the poor. I might not be able to celebrate each fall when a dozen poor village kids in Belize get to go to high school for free. I might not be comfortable in what some call the "dangerous" parts of town.

If it sounds like I'm bragging, I don't mean to. I mean to highlight the opportunities God gives all of us to change the world ... as long as we're willing to start tearing down the walls that separate us from it.

The Ripples of the Great Commission

All of this—tragedy on the Italy trip, the walls we surround ourselves with, and the junkyard memories I can't shake—all of this is why you're holding this book. When you wrestle with God for long enough, you can start to doubt your sanity—and even believe the easy answers that fly in from all sides about wealth and money:

Your wealth is God's way of showing that he approves of you and is blessing you.

Go and sell all your possessions and give the money to the poor, and you will have treasure in heaven.

All of this is above your pay grade—just keep tithing faithfully and don't sweat the details.

It's tempting to believe those answers. But I believe they're *all* wrong, at least for me. Yet I also believe that God doesn't want to hang me out to dry, with no viable options for how to live. He wants me to abide in Jesus and live the way Jesus lived. It sounds corny, but God wants me to make a difference in the world—and not primarily with my money, but with my *life*.

Think about the trajectory of your life up to this point. Often we end up back where we started, somewhere we never expected, or both. I think that's part of what Eliot is chasing when he writes that "We shall not cease from exploration / And the end of all our exploring / Will be to arrive where we started / And know the place for the first time."[3]

---

[3] T.S. Eliot, "The Four Quartets," Little Gidding, V.

11

That circular nature of life has a lot to do with the way this book is structured. In these pages, I tell my story in a series of "ripples" that spread across the world, along the way touching a wide variety of people and places.

This structure is also inspired by the "other" Great Commission we read in Acts 1. Matthew 28 is the famous version, where the risen Jesus tells his disciples, "All authority in heaven and on earth has been given to me. Therefore go and make disciples of all nations, baptizing them in the name of the Father and of the Son and of the Holy Spirit, and teaching them to obey everything I have commanded you. And surely I am with you always, to the very end of the age."

Rarely do we talk about the other version, though, where Jesus uses the image of concentric circles to describe how the power of the gospel will spread around the world. Listen to this: "But you will receive power when the Holy Spirit comes on you; and you will be my witnesses in Jerusalem, and in all Judea and Samaria, and to the ends of the earth" (Acts 1:8).

Picture that. Jerusalem first, then the surrounding territory, then eventually expanding to the whole of the known world. Jesus is describing a bull's-eye on a target. Or better, he's describing a stone dropped into a pond, from which increasingly larger circles radiate.

Like that imagined stone, any single life ripples outward. But for that to begin, we need to take a leap of faith.

This book is a record of how I've tried—how I'm still trying—to do exactly that. To dismantle the walls that separate and insulate me from the poor. It's a daily struggle. I haven't solved the problem of following Jesus as a wealthy Westerner. Rather, I'm wrestling with that tension. Embracing it.

In the following ripples of my story—
    from Southeast Asia
        to Central America
            to the Bay Area
                and all the way back again—

I'm inviting you to do the same. To join me in a leap of faith. There will be adventure, tragedy, and joy, and sometimes it will be hard to tell them apart. It's a journey of intentionally seeking out people who are different and ideas that are different, a journey of challenging presuppositions and being willing to live transparently. It's a journey about what wealth and poverty actually are and what they mean.

To be honest, I don't know where it will lead.

What I do know is that it has been incredibly enriching—far more so than any life lived for wealth or comfort or prestige could ever be.

It is also *shockingly* challenging. That's just another of those tensions for you.

One Last Thought before We Begin …

I wrote some of these stories on a warm spring day in Santa Barbara. Midmorning, a hummingbird buzzed through the open door and perched on the ceiling lamp. I stared at her for a long moment, wondering what she thought of the room and of the strange creature watching her. I marveled at the power thrumming through her tiny body.

Then—*zip*—she was gone, back through the door and into the garden.

A smile came to my face, unbidden. Open doors can bring us surprises that are beautiful and brimming with joy.

We should open more doors in our lives.

I'm not talking about metaphorical doors that let "potential" into our lives. I'm talking about *actual* doors. The doors to our houses and churches and businesses.

Yet in fear we lock doors. Shutter windows. Thicken walls. To what end? While we may protect ourselves from hummingbirds, we cannot ward away evil. Tragedy is no respecter of our defenses.

One reason I am writing this book is to ask: What if God is waiting to meet us when the rich and poor enter into relationships with each other?

Jesus tells a story of a rich man who planned a feast, but when the privileged guests failed to arrive, the host threw open the doors. He sent his servants out into the worst parts of the city to find guests. It's true this paints a picture of God's eternal kingdom, but it also speaks to our lives right here, right now. We're being offered tastes of that perfect feast at a banquet table filled with wonderful and different friends.

But we need to accept the invitation.

That's good news, whether you grew up in a junkyard, a backyard, or with no yard.

I'm trying to live with the doors of my heart open to the lives of people different than me. If tragedy and evil are givens, at least let a hummingbird in flight delight me. At least let there be no barriers between my own heart and the suffering of others.

Doesn't that sound wonderful? A bit too wonderful, to be honest.

Because when you live in one of the wealthiest places on earth, and following Jesus leads you to a slum in Bangkok, you know what happens? The same thing that happens when your daughter's close friend dies for no reason.

Your easy answers and presumptions get shot to hell.

~2~

FIRST RIPPLE: BANGKOK
AND SINGAPORE

If the city of Bangkok were a target, the Klong Toey slum would be right near the bull's-eye—but few people would aim for it.

Built on swampy land near a port on the Chao Phraya River, Klong Toey is home to more than one hundred thousand people, all of whom live in roughly *one* square mile. To put that in some perspective, the population density of New York City is less than a quarter of that.

The outer ring of the slum is typical of any hectic global city. The streets are clogged with honking cars and skittering motorbikes. Mom-and-pop shops sell regional foods and mobile phones and magazines. Ads for Coke and Krong Thip cigarettes compete with signs for drunken noodles and Chinese beers.

It is only when you turn down an alley and enter Klong Toey proper that you enter a different world.

The commercial trappings of the surrounding capital disappear by degrees. Less cement, more corrugated metal. Neon signs are replaced by cardboard cutouts with hand lettering. Since twisting passages are often so narrow that two people have to scoot past each other, the only vehicles—of which there are only a few—are small motorbikes. Buildings are built flush with other buildings, on top of other buildings, and on top of buildings that have fallen down. A single sheet of plywood is a generous wall. Sometimes a wall is simply a scrap of sheet metal leaned against a chain-link fence. Or just the fence.

The best bits of construction material look as if they were taken from my father's junkyard, while the worst bits aren't even building material. They're closer to litter.

These aren't buildings people should live in. They ought to be torn down. Except people are desperate, and Klong Toey keeps growing as more and more rural Thais come to Bangkok looking for elusive jobs and a better life.[4]

The areas wide enough to be actual streets have railroad tracks running down the center. Not all abandoned tracks either. Trains rumble past at regular intervals, their cars clearing the corrugated roofs and walls by mere inches.

Because of the constant, muggy heat—average temperatures are above eighty year-round, and in some months it rains more than half the days—windows and doors are always open. The residents share the mostly pointless quest for a breeze with feral cats, large rats, and the occasional extra-large python that slithers up from below. (Luckily I never encountered one—me and Indiana Jones both hate snakes.)

If you happen upon a nicely finished building that is constructed with something substantial, it is one of three things: a government building, a relief agency, or a church. And if you're Western, absolutely everyone you pass—sitting in a doorway, crouched beside a moped, leaning out through a window and into the alley—will stop what they're doing and stare.

I discovered these things about Klong Toey[5] when I was in Thailand with my daughter, Rachel. She's conversational in Thai, and she

---

[4] Another 863 million people live in similar slums and shantytowns around the globe. http://www.who.int/gho/urban_health/en/

[5] I was mostly in Lok 3. Other sections of Klong Toey may have a few concrete houses in a row, right across the path from the worst sheds. There are so many nuances. Some in Klong Toey are "career" slum-dwellers, who make their money on and in the slum, yet who continue to reside there as "well off." Others, perhaps next door, continue to be desperate for their next meal. It's almost like a microcosm of the globe.

runs an anti-trafficking organization called The SOLD Project.[6] Since she was in charge of our itinerary in Bangkok, I didn't get my marching orders for the day until my phone buzzed. *Fantastic change of plans*, read her text. *We're getting a tour of the slum.*

No river cruise around Bangkok then? So much for a leisurely day as a tourist.

To be honest, wandering around a stifling slum isn't my idea of a fun afternoon. But it makes the cut for my daughter—and my son, for that matter.

I have a vivid memory of Jedd, back when he was just a kid, riding on the back of a local guide in Belize. Jedd was in awe of being carried through a rainforest by someone wielding a machete in one hand and a shotgun in the other. My kids grew up taking trips like that every year, and it changed something inside of them. They came to view themselves as citizens of the world. D'Aun and I learned not to be surprised when one of our kids traveled to Ghana or Mumbai.

That was how I found myself turning away from the chaos and noise outside of Klong Toey and walking with my daughter into a different kind of chaos.

As we navigated the narrow spaces, I guessed the splintered posts and rusting frames were like petri dishes of various tropical diseases. Luckily it wasn't a scorching day, or the smells would have been overpowering. Countless meals being prepared on propane stoves. Mildew and an undertone of urine. Tobacco. Mesh bags filled with hundreds of live frogs—and tables covered edge-to-edge with skinned specimens.

Privacy seemed nonexistent. Bedrooms shared thin walls with the bedrooms next door. Kitchens and living rooms opened directly onto the street. Nearly everything I'd normally imagine happening indoors was happening in public instead. Space in the slum is too precious to devote to commerce, so there are no conventional shops or stores.

---

[6] Visit thesoldproject.com to learn more.

Commerce is conducted on doorsteps, through open windows, and hand to hand in the alleys.

If you live in the slum, you know your neighbors' business and they know yours. It's unavoidable when you've heard each other arguing through plywood walls or just outside the open window. People hook up, break up, and make up—often at full volume.

Deep inside Klong Toey, it hit me: poverty has an odor. The odor isn't the people who are poor, but poverty itself. It's a scent that's raw and untamed, pervasive and depressing. Yet it hints at potential power.

In a way, the scent of Klong Toey reminded me of how Dad smelled when he came home from a long day at the junkyard. Always a touch of grease, a touch of body odor, and the piss-and-vinegar attitude of a man who, for the sake of his family and the sake of his pride, wasn't afraid to just outwork everyone else. Klong Toey was a bit like that.

But just a bit. Because there was something else in the air, something that never clung to Dad.

I suspect it was hopelessness.

Meeting the Barkers

Rachel and I arrived at an open doorway in a tiny alley, indistinguishable from everything else we'd passed. It was a home and a mission.

Anji and Ash Barker, both Australians, moved to Klong Toey in 2002 with an organization called Urban Neighbours of Hope. Actually, they *were* the organization. Their founding principle was simple: by living in a slum, in essentially the same conditions as everyone around them, they could be good neighbors, and by being good neighbors they could give people hope. So they'd arrived with a five-year-old daughter, purchased a four-room house that was about four hundred square feet, and set about living as slum dwellers. They struggled with the language, the heat, the completely foreign culture, and about a million other things.

A dozen years later, some of those things were still struggles, but some weren't. Their daughter was going to an international high school in Bangkok, and their son—born the year they arrived—was at ease in the slum. They'd added two local foster kids to the family, learned the language, and become part of the community. Not that the Barkers "blended in" with the locals. Not at all. Anji was one of the only blondes in the entire slum, while Ash's rugby-player physique was impossible to miss in the small rooms and narrow alleys.

Anji and Ash told us stories. Endless stories of lives ground down beneath the weight of poverty. Like a boy growing up with foster parents, blind in one eye, because his teenage mom had an STD when she gave birth to him. Like a girl who should be in middle school but instead was raising her two younger siblings by herself. She didn't have a dad, her mom was in jail, and her grandmother started drinking every day at breakfast. Or a man with no control of his mind or bowels who smeared feces into his hair and onto his skin, then wandered in and out of people's homes. Or a woman who overdosed on glue fumes and needed to be chained to her own refrigerator in order to stay safe. Or a father who had sex with his daughter—and who allowed *his* father to have sex with her as well.

Not to mention all the regular run-of-the-mill jerks, the ones who hooked children on drugs and crushed families with loans that had 30 percent interest rates.

It was the world's most depressing lecture. I listened, fidgeting, to the narrative of extreme systematic poverty and how it ruins families and individual behaviors. How it narrows choices to bad and even worse. If it weren't for Anji and Ash's gallows humor—which they'd certainly earned the right to—it would have been unbearable.

The stories we heard were heartbreaking. Not because they were so awful, though they were. The real tragedy is that their awfulness is incredibly common.[7]

I'm not going to put numbers to everything, but consider the particular case of trafficking in Thailand, where one out of every *fourteen* children will be exploited for forced labor or forced sex.

---

[7] Did you just wonder, *My God,* how *common?* If so, consider chucking this book and reading *Walking With the Poor* by Bryant Myers. Perhaps God is stirring your heart to do something different.

Bangkok is a wealthy global city. It is also a slum city. And what happens in Bangkok is what happens anywhere the extremely rich coexist with the extremely poor: exploitation. That's one of those words that can hide certain realities. We normally apply the word to natural resources or to unfairly taking advantage of a situation. When we talk about the exploitation in Thailand, though, we have to combine these meanings.

I think about what the Barkers have done in Klong Toey. Organized soccer teams for the local kids. Established a handicraft business that now employs more than fifty people at double the local minimum wage. Raised money to rebuild the local school. Driven kids hours to visit parents who are in jail, several times a month, so that they can still be a family when the parents are released. The list of good done and mercy shown goes on and on—longer even than the list of evil I wrote about earlier.

The contributing factors to human trafficking are many: exploitation of the poor, the demand for prostitution, religious and social norms, corruption. But it was during my time in Klong Toey that my daughter highlighted another cause.

"*Poverty* is the trafficker."

She's surely right. If a sick mother could access a health clinic, her dutiful daughter would not need to sell her body to get money for medicine—nor would a thousand permutations of that same story need to occur.

So here's what I'm wrestling with. We could clone the Barkers and send a thousand of them into Klong Toey. And I wish we would! But if Rachel is right, and poverty is the trafficker, *children will continue to be trafficked.*[8]

---

[8] Now if we *actually* sent one thousand Barkers into Klong Toey, that really would make a difference—they'd probably figure out how to employ the entire slum. Trouble is, we've got a limited supply of Barkers, and there seems to be an endless supply of evil.

It's the age-old problem of treatment versus prevention. Think about the trans-Atlantic slave trade in the nineteenth century. The Underground Railroad helped escaped slaves reach free states in the US, but without the work of the Clapham Sect and William Wilberforce in Britain to cut off the supply of slaves, the Underground Railroad would have been doing the work of Sisyphus.

Solutions have to start at the source of economic need. And that source is often in the slum and rural regions of countries like Thailand, where young girls and boys are enticed by the stories of jobs and opportunity only to be coerced into sexual slavery or forced labor.

Writing in Raffles

When I first drafted these words about Klong Toey, just days after visiting my daughter, I was sitting at the Writers Bar, tucked into a corner of the lobby at the five-star Raffles Hotel in Singapore. Kipling, Hemingway, and Maugham had all sat there long before me.

Well-dressed and well-heeled guests crisscrossed the lobby. Families, all smiles and laughter, headed for the pool or a day of sightseeing. The phrase "my pleasure" constantly fell from the lips of the staff. I filled pages and pages of my spiral notebook, using the complimentary hotel pen.

I'd been picked up at my gate at the Singapore airport by someone from the hotel. She'd driven me in a golf cart to a private immigration control line. Only a few minutes later, she met me at the curb with my luggage, just as a Mercedes purred to a stop to take me to the hotel. On the drive into the city, I counted three Ferraris and two Lamborghinis racing past in the other direction. Singapore's peerless skyline reared up ahead of us, including the most expensive casino in the world and the hauntingly beautiful singing trees. Sprinkled everywhere were the gracious white colonnades of colonial-era British architecture.

At the Raffles, I'd approached the majestic, three-story entrance where turbaned Sikh doormen—dressed in impeccable white military uniforms with gold epaulets and black sashes—welcomed me through the doors. Instead of checking me in at the front desk, a charming employee walked me to the bar, ordered me a Singapore Sling, and helped me fill out my registration paperwork. Then we walked across the stunning lobby, past the billiard room, out through a garden, and finally to my spacious room. After pointing out the amenities at my disposal, he'd given me his personal card and urged me to call him if I needed anything.

Singapore and Klong Toey—same planet, different worlds. What did it mean that I'd been in both within the same week?

Sitting in the Writers Bar, looking over the first draft of what I'd written about the slum the Barkers called home, I took a drink of my overpriced Cabernet Sauvignon. Then I was struck by a profound thought.

I'm already forgetting the poor.

Which was quickly followed by another brilliant insight.

Crap, not again.

The Amnesia of Wealth

Safely away from the dangers and horrors of Klong Toey, I'm surrounded by luxury. Everything is comfortable, and everyone I meet wants me to be even *more* comfortable. I'd enjoy nothing more than to simply forget what I saw. Forget the pain and suffering, forget the sense of almost total hopelessness. I'd love to learn something—or fund something—and then move on. Back to my real life.

The feeling is unmistakable: I'm already slipping into the amnesia of wealth.

But should I forget? Can I move on? Should I?

There's a verse in the New Testament that gets a lot of airtime. "For God so loved the world …"

You probably know the rest, whether or not you grew up in church: "that he gave his one and only Son, that whoever believes in him shall not perish but have eternal life."

The familiarity of that verse disguises its plain meaning. In the Goble paraphrase, it would be something like, "God's love for the world was so great that it drove him to take drastic action to save it."

First God loved, then God acted.

Which is why it's so strange to read John 3:16 in the light of something else John wrote: "Do not love the world or anything in the world" (1 John 2:15).

John gives us a reason, or maybe a threat: Don't love the world, he says, because "if anyone loves the world, love for the Father is not in them."

So let me get this straight. First, God loves the world. Loves it so much, in fact, that he set in motion a plan to save the whole damned thing and everyone in it, all the way from Klong Toey to Singapore. Then God, through Scripture, tells the people he's saving that *they* can't love the world or anything in the world. Because if they do, it proves they aren't filled with God's love.

According to John, it sounds like if *we* do the very same thing *God* does—love the world—we're off the mark. That seems like it makes . . . very little sense.

Is it a cosmic case of "do as I say, not as I do"? Did the author not realize the contradiction? Or is something else going on here?

Sometimes life feels like I'm living it on a wrestling mat. Maybe if I could just pick a side. Give it all away for the sake of the poor—or just stop all this hand-wringing and start to enjoy the ride. Trouble is, neither way feels like the right path. Honestly, neither path feels like the *godly* path, at least for me. Hence the many times life—and God—seems to grab me in a headlock.

Let me be blunt about something. I almost said "confess" something, except that I don't think I have anything to confess. But what I'll be blunt about is this: when I'm in Klong Toey, I don't feel "called" to move there and minister to the poor. But the feeling goes beyond that. It's closer to a feeling that *it would be* wrong *for me to follow the example of the Barkers.*

How can that be?

How can it be wrong to love people no one else will love?

I don't know, to be honest. But I'm inclined to believe that God calls us to follow him individually and relationally.

God gives all of his children the same *what*. We're told to act justly, to love mercy, and to walk humbly with God. To love God and our neighbors with all our heart, soul, mind, and strength.

But when it comes to the *how*, I suspect God says to each of us, "Consider how I created you, because I made you that way for a reason."

I don't believe the answer to my questions, to my wrestling, is to try to be the next Saint Francis, just as I don't believe it is making sure I stay at every one of the world's top ten hotels.[9] That's the tension I've been wrestling with the whole of my adult life.

If you're reading this, there's a good chance you're nodding along. Because otherwise you would have already sold everything and moved to a slum—either that or this book would be an unopened paperweight on your mahogany shelf.

We are, in the words of Anne Frank, bundles of contradictions. And in real life—especially a life spent trying to follow Jesus—those contradictions aren't likely to go anywhere.

Like, I'm a wealthy American, sitting at the Writers Bar in Singapore's Raffles Hotel.

I'm the father of a Thai-speaking daughter who is determined to end sex trafficking and a son who's trying to change the world with art.

I'm a member of a nondenominational Protestant megachurch in the Bay Area.

I consistently try to break down the walls between myself and the poor, from the city where I live to the other side of the world.

I own a six-figure sports car.

So which is the real me? Search me—you should probably ask D'Aun, since she's the one who puts up with me the most, in all my knuckleheadedness.

With all my contradictions, all my wrestling, I keep chasing something that's almost ephemeral. A "third way," I could call it, between wealth and poverty, between forgetting and remembering. It's a winding

---

[9] I'll tell you a story about this in chapter 4. Spoiler alert: I don't come out looking great.

way, tracing a path between a love in John 3:16 that acts to save a broken world and a faith in 1 John 2:15 that refuses to love the world or anything in it.

I pray it's God's way too, though to claim that with a straight face, I'd have to be nearly insane.

Blissful Ignorance?

A friend once wrote, "Poverty is not simply about lack of cash, but a lack of hope to believe the life God intends for us is possible."[10]

That's certainly true in a place like Klong Toey. Pick a random resident and give them sufficient cash to move themselves, their family, outside the slum. Enough cash to start a business, or go to trade school, or pay off the loan sharks. A lack of cash can cripple, but with an extra boost, many of them would start to follow longtime dreams. Yet some wouldn't—not because they lack cash, but because they lack sufficient hope to imagine a better future. Cash without corresponding hope can be worse than useless.

The New Testament talks a great deal about both cash and hope, and sometimes how the two go together. Paul, writing to people living in Galatia, recalls a conversation with some influential Christian leaders. They wanted to vet him, which wasn't a bad instinct, considering a few years before he was the guy rounding up Christians and throwing them in jail. The upshot of their talk is this: "All they asked was that we should continue to remember the poor, the very thing I had been eager to do all along" (Gal 2:10).

That's stunning. The only thing Paul was asked to do, by way of proving his *bona fides* as a follower of Jesus, was to continue to remember the poor. That's *it?*

You can read Paul's response a couple of ways. *Saint* Paul, the guy with the halo, agrees with the request in a prissy voice, patting himself on the back the whole time. But Paul the pushed-around, the guy

---

[10] The friend happens to be Ash Barker, and if you've never read his books *Make Poverty Personal* or *Risky Compassion*, you should.

25

who's burning with God's Spirit after being struck blind by that same Spirit—he's writing with emotion. Less like Scripture, and more like an email to a friend: *Can you* believe *those numbskulls—the only thing they asked me to do was the thing I was* already *doing!*

That was certainly good news to the poor. Because "remember the poor" meant more than tossing some coins their way. It also meant they would be prayed for, talked about, advocated for. Treated as people, in other words, and not projects.

That sounds like good news to me as well. I'm rich, true, but I'm eager to remember the poor. I believe I'm doing the right thing a lot of the time. I wouldn't be writing this book if I wasn't regarded by my peers as a leader in this area. And I definitely wouldn't be writing it if, in my heart, I felt like a hypocrite.

Together, D'Aun and I have built Jaguar Creek Research & Education Center, which helps to both protect the environment and train a new generation of educators in Belize. I chair the board for Path-Light International, which provides hope through faith and learning for at-risk students in rural Belize. I serve on the board and the diversity committee at Westmont College, as well as on the board at The SOLD Project. I'm part of the advisory councils of 24–7 Prayer International and Fuller Seminary School of Intercultural Studies. Our family foundation supports children's homes, youth programs, vocational training in Haiti, a shelter for abused women, and the Old Skool Cafe.[11] It also funded a collegiate center for global learning.

If Christian leaders wanted to vet me, and "all they asked was that we should continue to remember the poor," I'd come out looking pretty good.

Unfortunately for my peace of mind, Jesus doesn't ask me to look good or to be better than some of my peers—he asks me to follow him. And "follow" needs to be an ongoing verb, even when the amnesia of wealth suggests a rest stop.

---

[11] Which I'll tell you about in chapter 6.

It reminds me of when Jesus told a story about forgetting the poor. We call it the parable of the Good Samaritan, and you can read it in Luke 10.

You probably know the outline: a lawyer asks Jesus what he has to do in order to live forever, and Jesus tells him to love God with everything he's got, and also to love his neighbor. Then the lawyer gets technical on Jesus and asks for a definition of "neighbor." So Jesus tells a story in which a guy gets beat up, and the usual suspects who *should* help him—the good guys of society—decide to pass him by like he's invisible. Then the twist: one of the injured man's natural enemies sees him, and rather than finishing him off, he gets the injured man back to the city and then pays for his recovery. Then Jesus whacks the lawyer upside the head with the damning rhetorical question: *Which one was a true neighbor to the injured man?*

I can picture the lawyer looking at the dirt when he grudgingly answers, "The one who had mercy."

There's something I find interesting—or perhaps troubling—in Jesus's final words in this story. "Go and do likewise." Go and do the same thing the Good Samaritan does, the same thing Paul was eager to do.

Remember the poor.

Help the helpless.

Why is that troubling? Mostly because it sounds so *un*like what we usually hear in our churches and small groups and in the latest Christian books. If it's true that the path to eternal life starts, and proceeds, *through* this present life, then what happens when I'm a "good Christian" but forget the poor and my neighbor? What happens if everything I do for the poor isn't enough, or if it isn't even the primary thing God is asking of me?

One thing I've learned is that it's all too easy to forget the poor—*especially when we think we're remembering them.*

I can say, with honesty, that I know more about Klong Toey and the people who live there than 99.9 percent of other Westerners. My wealth gives me the ability to travel to Bangkok and learn about them, just as I've traveled to other slums from Haiti to Zimbabwe. But so what? I don't stay in Bangkok. That's not *my* job. Staying in Bangkok is what people like the Barkers do, or what my kids might do. So I fly back home.

Then when I get back home, and back to being comfortable, my wealth gives me the option of forgetting the poor who live *near* me. What good am I then? For all my knowledge of Klong Toey, am I really any better off, in a kingdom sense, than some wealthy Westerner living in blissful ignorance?

For most of us, the poor aren't forgotten in dramatic, easy-to-retell events. *Let me tell you the crazy story of that one time I forgot the poor,* said no one ever. We forget the poor through the small, insidious, cumulative decisions we make on a daily basis.

I know that's how it works for me.

Focusing social energy on certain people at the expense of other people. Buying *this* instead of *that* simply to project a successful image. Building relationships with those who can help me in obvious ways—like socially or financially—rather than with people who can help me spiritually or in other ways. I could go on and on.

Ironically, I'm most likely to forget the poor when I forget my own wealth.

I've insensitively worn my Rolex to a village meeting in Belize. I've stupidly chatted about an upcoming vacation to Europe with a woman who has never left her neighborhood. Upon hearing about a need in a community, I've impatiently thrown money at the problem and mentally moved on to the next task while the poor around me stare. In these and a thousand other small acts of forgetting, I have objectified the poor. Because I have not considered their lives, their context, and instead imposed my own, I have forgotten them. Face-to-face with the poor, even as I've "helped" them, I have forgotten.

For heaven's sake, I get upset when the airline app isn't working properly on my iPhone. Or when the waiter brings me a medium steak after I ordered medium rare. I can even be irritated when my new shoes squeak too loudly. I can be the living definition of the idiot complaining about First-World problems.

In the midst of it all, I forget the poor.

And when I forget the poor, I forget God. The equation is that simple—and that damning.

Remember how Ash said that poverty is about a lack of cash *and* a lack of hope? Sometimes I think wealth isn't simply about an excess of cash, but also about an excess of *hope*. See, wealth makes it possible for me to hope that the life and the lifestyle I *want* for myself is possible. Deserved, even. That excess of selfish hope makes it possible for me to love the world and the things in it. And when I do that, it doesn't matter how much money I give away or how many boards I serve on. The love of God is not in me.

All wealthy people fall prey to this. Some of us are learning to catch ourselves and change the way we're acting. Or even repent. Some of us remain clueless.

Sometimes it's really hard to tell the difference.

~3~

SECOND RIPPLE: BELIZE AND HAITI

Back in the early nineties I wanted to buy a tropical island. Not for the stereotypical reason of owning my own slice of paradise, however. I just wanted to freak out D'Aun.

The idea came to me as I was scanning the real estate section of the *Wall Street Journal*.[12] Perusing the listings gave me a sense for who was doing what in the market, which helped us make better decisions at Goble Properties. But tucked in a corner of the international listings, a small item caught my eye. "Island for sale. Belize, Central America." Mostly thinking about scaring my wife—"Honey, we're moving to Belize!"—and partly wondering if it might be a good investment location, I wrote away for information.

A week later, I dropped a stack of paper as thick as a phonebook onto my desk and began to educate myself.

The top ten pages were about the island, which I instantly dismissed as overpriced and ridiculous—especially for what amounted to a practical joke. Belize was cheap, but a tropical island was still a tropical island.

However, the next several inches of information about Belize fascinated me. Belize wasn't one of those Central American countries I might have at least pretended to know something about, like Costa Rica. As I scanned the pages, I learned that Belize was tiny. Surrounded by Mexico, Guatemala, and the Caribbean Sea, it was only 180 by 70 miles. Home to less than two hundred thousand residents

---

[12] That dates me—I was alive when people read newspapers.

at the time—a mix of Mayan, Spanish, former Caribbean slaves, Mexican, and British—it was the only country in Central America whose official language was English. And because it was so small, in only a few miles a traveler could transition from turquoise water and white sand into some of the densest, least developed tropical rainforest in the world.

The information was a sales pitch for investors: Belize was safe, stable, and growing. Since I already knew how to invest in real estate in California, how hard could it be to replicate that in Belize? I'd learn a few things about the government and economy, figure out the best way to approach the local markets, and start turning a profit. Naïve perhaps, but it was still worth a short visit.

I was already planning to go to a Christian management conference in Dallas with my pastor, so I gave him a call.

"Hey, do you have a few extra days after the conference?"

"Maybe, Roy—why, what's up?"

"I want to take a little side trip."

"Like to Austin or something?"

"Something like that. Ever heard of Belize?"

We ended up crisscrossing the country from north to south, scouting for investment opportunities. And ... there weren't any. Belize was high-risk as far as Goble Properties was concerned.

However, as I was driving up the Hummingbird Highway and thinking about how gorgeous the country was, and contemplating whether God had led me to this place—and if so, why—it struck me that I might be looking at things through the wrong lens.

The goal of *investing* wasn't the wrong lens, but maybe the *object* of that investment was wrong. I experienced a pith helmet moment: *Belize could be an amazing opportunity—not for my business, but for ministry.*

At the time, D'Aun and I were running a small Christian camp at a lake property we owned in the Sierras. We were passionate about sharing what was (then) an almost unheard-of idea: that Scripture calls us to care for the earth. After seven years, we had a strong and dedicated group of folks who wanted to do more, and it began to dawn on me that it might be possible to use the base of support from the camp to launch a movement in the wider Christian community.

Maybe, just maybe, Belize could be the first step toward thinking globally, not just locally, about how God might want us to be good stewards of creation. What if we created another camp, but this time in the rainforest?

Three months later, I was landing at the Belize International Airport again, but this time with D'Aun, the kids, and my mother. With unspoiled rainforest in Belize going for almost nothing,[13] we were able to begin the process of purchasing what would come to be called Jaguar Creek.

What surprises me about this story is that my willingness to ask questions—even questions about buying an island for a joke—led to a real opportunity to do good. Sure, I was a rich young entrepreneur with a crazy sense of humor. No argument there. And once I'd moved on from my joke, my next idea was to make a profit in the foreign real estate market. Not wrong, but also not the subject we're wrestling with here.

Yet it was that somewhat wandering, idiosyncratic path that led me to an unexpected opportunity to invest in the poor by helping to steward the environment.

Funny phrase, isn't it—*invest in the poor?*

As a real estate investor, I invest in order to get something in return. Profits, primarily, along with the knowledge that a successful business investment can be good for the surrounding community in terms of jobs, infrastructure, and so on.

That's why investing in the *poor* sounds odd, because we aren't used to thinking of the poor as being able to give something in return.

In fact, however, the poor have *abundant* things they are capable of giving—which is exactly why investing in the poor can seem

---

[13] That isn't a figure of speech. It was like a hundred bucks an acre.

selfish. In crude terms, if the poor do produce a return on investment, doesn't that mean I'm investing in them for exactly the wrong reasons? I should do it because it's right, not because I want to get something in return.

In my life, I have certainly invested in the poor for the wrong reasons. I've done it for recognition, or out of duty, or simply out of habit. But those things can only take you so far. Willpower is a finite resource when it comes to following Jesus. Willing yourself to obey works until it doesn't.

My prayer—more like a desperate wish, really—is that some spark of something in my soul is telling me that investing in the poor isn't what I do to get a return, but what I do to stay *alive*.

That may not make much sense. It may not even be true. But I want it to be true, and a major theme in the story of my life is looking for evidence of that.

Screwups

The rich get a bad rap—and sometimes deservedly. We make mistakes that have very real consequences. Our actions can increase the amount of suffering and selfishness in the world. Our influence is proportional to our wealth, and thus it is disproportional.

The poor, however, get a pretty *good* rap—at least the poor who live across the world from us.[14] We tend to label poor people as industrious, patient, and victimized. We can view them as virtuous, even when we know nothing about them.

But let's be real. We should *all* get a bad rap.

If we're going to wrestle with what it means to follow Jesus in a stratified global society, we need to start with honesty. Because we're all human, we're all screwups. That's our natural state. You don't become a screwup when you cross a certain level of income. The rich just have more opportunities to screw up publicly and prodigally.

---

[14] The poor who live across town from us? Not so much.

Here's an example of what I'm talking about. Early on in our time at Jaguar Creek, we began to look at ways to help develop the surrounding villages. They were incredibly isolated, not just from each other but from the rest of the country. We hoped that Jaguar Creek could become a good neighbor and be a positive influence in the region.

Belize is a place where no major nonprofits operate, mostly because they don't see it as a good place to deploy their funds. It's simply too small and too different. It doesn't fit into a natural category like "Caribbean Basin" or "Central America" or "Latin America." So launching a ministry in Belize is like launching a one-off branch office with a very small target audience—not worth it to larger organizations. As one executive of World Vision once told me, there are more than 1,500 cities in the world with larger populations than the whole of Belize, so if they're going to open a new office, it'll be where they can do the most good.

Belize, therefore, gets overlooked. In the absence of big players, however, there are dozens of mom-and-pop organizations that stitch together the networks needed to sustain a country continually on the brink. Because even with all its virtues, Belize is still very poor.

This effort is good! Privileged people, mostly from America, are seeing various needs in Belize and trying to address them. They're trying to love the poor, and the size and scope of their efforts are appropriate to the country.

But it's also bad. (What's that, two major tensions already in this chapter? Three?) See, Belize has a reputation for being extremely "missions friendly." Speak English and have a few thousand bucks? Buy yourself some rainforest and start doing the work of the Lord! I jest, of course.[15] Kind of.

Because even though people don't need a license to do missions, they probably should. It's a lot like driving (and having children): you

---

[15] But not really. That's basically what we did too. Difference is, unlike the other guys, we did it the right way. Ahem.

can do a lot of unintentional damage if you don't know what you're doing.

Take me, for example. Early on in our time at Jaguar Creek, I led a small team to one of the nearby villages. We hopped in a van and bumped the four miles to Armenia Village.[16] Like most rainforest communities, this one had about five hundred people at the time— mostly Mestizo, with a few Mayans. They lived at a wide spot on the road in the middle of large swath of rainforest, with no electricity, no natural water source, and irregular bus service. The men mostly worked as subsistence farmers in small fields carved out of the forest or, when they could, at the large citrus plantations a few miles away. Sometimes they'd get a job out of the area and move. Sadly, they sometimes stayed away and never came back. The women stayed home, taking care of their children and homes, and perhaps cooking extra tortillas they might sell. The kids had a small school in the village to attend, but many dropped out.[17]

We sat down with several of the leaders—all men—from Armenia Village. Our meeting was in the community center, and since English was the second language of the locals, we got right to business without a lot of chitchat.

"I am told by one of our staff people," I began, "that you would like to build an area for washing clothes. A place where people could gather and talk as they scrubbed things clean. Tell me more."

"Yes. The women have to walk miles to the river now. Having something in the village would be wonderful."

Perfect: a project that would benefit everyone, bring real improvement to the village, and be fairly easy for us to build. Before we left, we asked them to make a drawing of what they wanted and submit a budget.

---

[16] Named for the refugees in Armenia because this Belizean village was also established as a place for refugees from the war-torn nations surrounding Belize.

[17] School through what we'd call eighth grade is compulsory, but the rules are not enforced well.

When I got the plans and budget I smiled. It amounted to a concrete basin for holding water, a drain, and a few raised benches. It was about fifteen feet by fifteen feet, big enough for three to four women at a time to wash. And the cost, mostly for the concrete, was minimal. *Wow, we can do so much with so little,* I thought. *If this is all they need to make life a little easier, we've got to do this.*

So I approved the project.

Several months later, I drove back to the village to check on the progress. The concrete basin was poured, but nobody was using it. Upon inspection I realized the drain would direct the water right into the school playground. And then I realized an even bigger flaw: there was no water source.

That's when the obvious slapped me upside the head: even if there were a cistern, *how would it ever be filled?*

We'd failed to make life any easier for the women. In fact, we'd made it harder. Instead of taking their laundry to the river, now they had to bring the river—one heavy, sloshing bucket at a time—to their laundry.

Embarrassing. But it fits our narrative, doesn't it? "Rich white man is a cultural knucklehead."

Except that's not the whole picture. See, the village leaders embarrassed themselves as well. I found out later they had never asked the women if they wanted the laundry center. They didn't.[18]

The Schemer and the Brute

The rich and the poor both make mistakes.

But let me turn the mirror on us, the wealthy. Most Westerners have good intentions. Most Christians have good intentions.

---

[18] And yes, I'm well aware of the moral of this story: ask the women if you want to get a job done right. That's not me being flippant. It's good missiology (and common sense) to hear from the whole community, not just a small group. When we ignore a whole section of any community, our mistakes are going to be magnified and our successes smaller. Study after study has shown that when you engage women in underrepresented communities, you create more lasting positive change.

Yet—allow me to tweak the adage here—the road to sucking at following Jesus is paved with good intentions.

For example? We can leave a missions trip with a smile even though we know that half of the men in the village we visited are unemployed. Or that the teenage girls will be looking for a husband instead of going to high school because they have no other future. It's not that we're smiling *at* those stark realities, or even that we're ignoring them. Far from it. Often we're working to *fix* those problems. Still, we can't help but smile, because even in the midst of all their issues, *the people just seem so joyful.*

That last line is a bit sarcastic, of course. And this whole paragraph is even more that way, so be sure to read it with your best sarcastic tone. *We, who have so much, are so unhappy much of the time. And the locals, who have so little, are so filled with joy. It's almost impossible not to smile at the beautiful lesson we're learning!*

I'm told I can be too sarcastic, so let me say it like this: there's simply no way we can know what's beneath the joy and contentment we see. Or *think* we see. When we fly in for two days, or two weeks, and then fly home, it's like looking at someone's life through a keyhole: we can see only a tiny fraction. We may learn facts, but we don't build deep relationships. We may *begin* relationships—don't hear me saying that cross-cultural relationships are impossible, because they're not—but there's no way we can know our new "friends" at the level of real life. There's no way that, after two weeks, we can come home and sum up a life with a single word or phrase.

After all, there are a host of things we don't hear about in our brief time together. Like the gnawing, daily fear of getting evicted. Or the husbands who decide to move away, or shack up with a teenager in the next village over. Or the constant fear of an illness that cannot be addressed because there is no basic health care.

Short-term trips typically give us nothing deeper than an edited version of a life, rather than the whole story, in all its glorious and gory details. It's the Facebook version of relating to the poor, where everyone presents to each other only those things that are acceptable in public. We click "like" and move on. The rich present their strength and compassion and curiosity, while the poor present their joy and patience in the face of suffering. Those things *may* be true of us, but they are not the full truth.

To make a sinfully trite comparison, when D'Aun and I have friends over for dinner, we don't begin the dinner conversation by asking how we can help them with their problems, just as we don't invite our guests into the messy laundry room. The poor treat their rich visitors the same way. We are treated to the best food, and we see the smiling kids around the table on their best behavior. We see what's working in the community, and we make a "difference."

Then we leave. And real life resumes.

I'm convinced that God is calling me to enter lasting relationships with the poor, rather than a) ignoring them or b) entering pretend relationships with them.[19]

But once I begin a relationship with someone, I'd better be prepared for dysfunction. For theirs, as they become comfortable sharing the full picture of their life. And for mine too, because nothing brings out my dysfunction like relationships with people who are different than me.

It reminds me of the story of Jacob and Esau we find in Genesis. If you want to talk about relational assumptions and personal dysfunction, just read a few chapters of *their* story.

Their mother, Rebekah, knows trouble is coming while they are still in the womb, because she can literally feel the twins fighting inside of her. An earnest prayer yields a less-than-comforting answer from God. When it's time to deliver, Esau is born first, covered in hair, followed by his smooth brother—who happens to be grasping his older brother's heel.

Father Isaac, the old redneck, loves Esau, because he sees in his oldest son a version of himself: strong, impulsive, and obsessed with

---

[19] Actually, I think God is calling *you* to that as well. But if I told you that outside of a footnote, you might stop reading.

hunting. Rebekah, on the other hand, loves Jacob, perhaps because of his intelligence and cleverness. And the brothers' relationship goes downhill pretty much from the start.

First Jacob tricks Esau into giving up his legal right to be recognized as the firstborn son—a move that will cost Esau dearly when Isaac passes away. Then Esau marries two foreigners, causing both of his parents grief. Then Rebekah helps Jacob trick her husband, who is on his deathbed, into giving Jacob the *blessing* of the firstborn as well. Esau, understandably in this cultural context, vows to kill his brother as soon as possible. Rebekah helps Jacob flee to his uncle's ranch, hoping that Esau will forget his grudge in time.

Having spent decades assuming the worst about each other, both brothers then spend the next few decades living in different countries.

You know what Jacob and Esau had in common? They both excelled at using other people. They were objectifiers extraordinaire. Jacob used his brother's appetites and passions to get what he wanted. Esau viewed his brother as nothing more than second born, refusing to see him as a person. Add up all the objectification and you get insurmountable walls between family members. You get brothers turned into strangers and enemies.

Jacob and Esau. The schemer and the brute.

In my life? I've been both, God help me.

The Global Church

Our world is increasingly globalized. That's so true it's a truism.

But people overlook that the first truly global institution was the church. Maybe it was the words of Jesus in Acts 1:8 we talked about in the last chapter, or maybe they were just crazy, but either way the apostles and their followers had a passion for going from their base in Jerusalem into Samaria, then Judea, and eventually to the ends of the known world. Paul even seemed to have a death wish to appear before Caesar and share the gospel. These folks thought big, and the result was a globalized faith.

(Here's why starting in Samaria is so important, by the way: the apostles had been raised to hate the people who lived in Samaria. The parable of the Good Samaritan told by Jesus drew its power—and even shock value—from the fact that the injured man was ultimately saved by someone he despised. So the disciples' natural instinct would have been to skip over Samaria entirely and go straight to the rest of the world. Sort of like us locking our car doors to drive past a "bad" neighborhood to the airport … and then flying to Zimbabwe for a missions trip.)

The good news is that because the church is a global institution,[20] the church is in the perfect position to respond to a globalized world. From its founding, it was given both the mission and the power to go into all the world.

Personally, I try to obey that mandate. I travel frequently and widely. There's the Raffles Hotel I stay in, sure, but there are also bunk beds in jungles and flea-ridden mattresses in dive hotels.

But over and over I'm convicted by Acts 1:8—that to get from Jerusalem to the ends of the world, I've got to travel through Judea and Samaria. Not skip past certain places, or fly over them, but travel through them. Places where the people are different from me. Places my own culture has taught me to consider as lesser, or as unsafe. To despise, even.

If I gladly board a flight to Bangkok but hesitate to drive through a so-called dangerous area of my own town, I'll never understand the inherent flaws, weaknesses, gifts, or talents of my own culture—or anyone else's.

So what's a guy like me supposed to do?

Cross the divide.

It's that simple, and that impossible.

---

[20] When every branch of Christianity is added together, there are nearly 2.5 *billion* Christians. Globally, that's one out of every three people. Africa alone has more than half a billion Christians.

Because I seem to put up walls faster than I can take them down. Yeah, other people are putting up walls as well. That's true. But one thing I've observed about the physics of walls is that it's a lot easier to break down the walls other people make than to break down my own.

Welcome to Haiti

Head directly east from Belize, across the Caribbean Sea, and you hit the nation of Haiti.

In 1991, Lieutenant General Raoul Cedras staged a military coup in the nation of Haiti, overthrowing the government of Jean-Bertrand Aristide. The United States, along with other countries, put pressure on Cedras to step down and allow the elected ruler of the country to return. Cedras resisted. By 1994, the US was preparing to force Cedras out with a military intervention named, with typical bureaucratic creativity, Operation Uphold Democracy. A last-ditch US delegation traveled to Haiti, led by Senator Sam Nunn, former president Jimmy Carter, and General Colin Powell, and their mission succeeded. On October 15, 1994, Aristide returned to Haiti.

That same month, I flew into Port-au-Prince to connect with people doing effective community development work in the area. The nonprofit I was involved with was looking to partner with them in the wake of the government transition. We hoped to send them volunteers, because we knew the people on the ground in Haiti could identify real needs, create solid guidelines for engagement, and provide a meaningful experience that wasn't just more busywork for short-term missions teams.

Even while still inside the airport, I could tell the city was on the edge of chaos, tentatively held in check by the pervasive presence of US military personnel.[21]

As we traveled away from the airport, I got a briefing on the realities of life there. Eight in ten Haitians were bringing home less than

---

[21] Yes, I get the irony. Let's move on.

two dollars a day, and half were bringing home less than one dollar a day. Half of all children weren't enrolled in school. Haiti was the poorest country in the Western Hemisphere by a massive margin.[22]

What that meant on a practical level was that the people of Haiti were forced to make compromises and take risks and shortcuts. Deforestation is a prime example, and slapping together multistory buildings without proper engineering or construction materials is another.

No one in Haiti thought those were *good* ideas. It's just that no one had a choice.

While visiting with my hosts, I sat with people inside a church that had no roof, listening to their stories of the violence brought by Cedras's thugs.

I watched men squat in dry riverbeds, pounding rocks together to make sand, which they would scoop into bags and sell to a local cement factory for next to nothing.

I walked through the slum of Cite Soleil, where upwards of four hundred thousand people live, and I'd be lying if I said it didn't make Klong Toey look a whole lot better. That's a jackass kind of thing to say, but it's true. Picture roads literally paved with litter—scraps of tires, smashed bottles, and cardboard scraps so thick you can't see the dirt beneath. Imagine freestanding shacks made from sticks and rusty metal, scattered haphazardly around because every spot to build is as terrible and pointless as any other spot. Envision countless puddles, each a little dirtier and more poisoned than the last, formed when tropical rains flush the filth of poverty into the alleyways. In some ways it felt like the junkyard extended for miles, except that no one had to actually *live* in the junkyard.

Maybe if I'd met the Barkers of Haiti it would have been different. As it was, the suffering in Cite Soleil seemed unrelieved, hopelessness a total way of life.

---

[22] It still is.

As I walked down the alleys of Cite Soleil, kids walked over to me—not to beg, but simply to cling to my arms and legs. As if I might carry them to a better life. The mothers, hanging back from their children, did beg. For money, for food, for clothing—for anything that would help. And nearly anything would have helped, they were so destitute.

We talk about the unintentional harm in relief efforts, and rightly so. But that day, in that place, it felt like there was no way life could be worse. Like no unintentional harm could be worse than the harm these people were suffering simply by living each day in that place.

There were fathers there as well. They asked me for help, in their own way, just as the women and children did. "I need a job" and "I'm not sure I can feed my children" were said all too often. What made their suffering almost harder to bear was the embarrassment burning between us. They were so ashamed that they couldn't raise their eyes higher than my knees.

On my final day in Haiti, my hosts took me to downtown Port-au-Prince. The capital is a city of contrasts, blending poverty with old colonial architecture. The buzz of energy surprised me—I hadn't expected so much activity in a country that had just been occupied by the US military, and with a recently restored prime minister.

We were outside the presidential palace when I saw a beggar lying on the edge of the sidewalk. He was on his side, fetal. As we walked closer, I could see that his feet were deformed so severely that he couldn't stand or even walk. His only way of getting anywhere would be to crawl.

I wondered if there was anything I could do for him. Not much, I realized sadly.

Then I remembered the Haitian coins in my pocket. At least I could give him enough for his next meal. As I reached into my pocket, the man looked up at me, slowly raising one hand to accept the gift. My hand neared his, ready to drop the coins. And then I froze. His movement had turned his chest toward me, and I could read the comic sans writing across the front of his purple T-shirt:

Shop till you drop!

This man—this child of God—could do neither. All he could do was crawl across the sidewalks and city streets of the poorest city in the poorest country in the Western Hemisphere. All he could wear was a shirt that someone in the States had bought on impulse and then thrown away.

I dropped the coins into his open hand, my eyes glued to that damned T-shirt. And then I walked away, head spinning with guilt and irony and sadness.

I should have stopped and done more. I could have talked to him, found some way to comfort him. But I had a plane to catch and important meetings to attend. Someone else would help him more than I did, right? Of course someone would. It wasn't my job—*couldn't* be my job—so someone else must be ready to help him, after I left.

Several hours later I was boarding a flight to Miami, and from there to a meeting at a resort in the US Virgin Islands. By sheer coincidence, I sat next to the US ambassador to Haiti. He told me about fundraising goals and development targets. He used the word "synergy" more than once and allowed himself a smile about the progress taking place in the country since the successful conclusion of Operation Uphold Democracy. He never mentioned individual people, only percentages and demographics. Eventually I stopped listening.

When I finally got back to California, it was easy to remember the people I'd seen in Haiti. Mostly because every time I tried to eat, my food tasted like failure.

What was the point of going somewhere like Port-au-Prince, or Cite Soleil, if I wasn't going to do anything about it? Jesus commands his disciples to be his witnesses, and he promises them sufficient power in the form of the Holy Spirit. So why did I feel so powerless to help?

It's the kind of question that takes a lifetime to answer.

~4~

THIRD RIPPLE: CALIFORNIA

I sat in the dentist's office with the kind of carefree boredom that comes from being a healthy twenty-eight-year-old with the ability to pay for clean, healthy teeth. The dentist would undoubtedly make me wait for quite a while—before making me wait in another room while reclining on my back, no less—so I sorted through a pile of magazines, hoping to find a distraction.

A headline on a travel magazine caught my eye. *Top 10 Hotels in the World!*

Now *that* would get my mind out of this dingy office. I opened to the article and began to browse. As I flipped past picture after picture, I realized these hotels weren't just gorgeous ... they were familiar. A thought struck me, so I turned back to the beginning of the article. Paying closer attention, I began to count—and by the time I reached the end of the list, I was stunned to discover I'd stayed at seven of the ten hotels.

Stunned—but also, how cool was that! I wouldn't go around bragging about it, of course. I wasn't that kind of guy. But I could feel proud of my accomplishment. And if someone happened to ask me about it, well, it wouldn't be bragging to tell the truth.

Then another thought hit me: it would be fun to plan a vacation to complete the list. New York, London, then Rome. A mixture of ambition and competitiveness began prowling around my chest. I knew D'Aun would tell me our kids were too young for such a trip, or that the cost was too high, but eventually I'd convince her.

Smiling to myself, I closed the magazine and looked up. Drab drapes, scuffed wallpaper, and carpet worn thin by thousands of anxious feet. The waiting room was the antithesis of the hotels I'd just seen. And the people here were not the suave, happy travelers and business leaders I'd seen in the magazine. At best, they were passively waiting, like me. At worst they were hurting.

That's when something new stirred in my chest. *I've been to seven of the top ten hotels in the world, and I'm not even thirty?*

The thought no longer produced a feeling of pride. Instead it felt out of place or inappropriate. Almost *wrong.*

My parents grew up in the Great Depression. Dad told me stories of going without food as a kid, and Mom told me stories about her poor mining town in Oklahoma. For all of my childhood, my folks drove rebuilt cars and worked long hours. Dad had the calloused hands of a junkyard parts puller, and I knew my older brother, who was running the junkyard, still came home exhausted and covered in grease. Some of the junkyard employees—a few of whom I remembered from my time there and who were *still* pulling parts—earned less in a year than I did in a month.

And me? I'd been a "working man" for a whopping six years, or seven if you counted the deals I did from my dorm room my senior year. My skills and temperament were well suited to real estate investing and redeveloping older buildings. Escaping the junkyard had turned out to be a great move. Life was good. D'Aun and I were perpetually remodeling our rambling older home. Rachel and Jedd— three years and three months old, respectively—were happy and healthy. We drove nice cars, I had strong investments, we even owned lake property in the Sierras.

How in God's name did I deserve such luxury and opulence? How could somebody my age have already been to seven of the top ten hotels in the world?

But maybe those were the wrong questions. As I'd demonstrated with my life, such career success wasn't out of the realm of possibility. The right skill set, the right breaks early on, enough hard work and a good team … there were lots of people my age who made more than I did and who lived more luxurious lifestyles than I did.

Something deeper was bothering me, I realized—something more complicated and specific.

How in God's name could I enjoy such extravagance *while still following Jesus?*

Now *that* was a question to keep me busy for a lifetime.

People With Big Houses

That article about the world's ten best hotels changed me.

That's a pathetic conversion story, but it's what I've got. Not every life can sound like a *Readers' Digest* "Drama in Real Life." I've been different since that day. Call it what you want: guilt, self-awareness, the Holy Spirit.[23]

However you describe it, my life has changed. Because reading that article was what got me into wrestling. That's another way it isn't like a typical conversion story. You know how conversions usually go: "I once was lost and now am found, was blind but now I see." A switch gets flipped. There's before and then there's after. But it didn't work that way for me. (Maybe it doesn't for *most* of us.) For me it was the start of a lifelong wrestling match.

At the ripe old age of twenty-two, as I graduated from college, I'd already had an obvious and open door waiting for me to step through. And I did. I worked for Goble Properties. I won't say I was lucky, because it was a door that initially made it harder for me to follow God. But I will say that I had what a lot of people want: a challenging, satisfying job with a solid, growing paycheck.

At the even riper age of twenty-eight, though, life suddenly looked different. It was less inevitable. More complicated. Wealth complicated it, for sure—but I'm talking about the complications of grappling with what my life could or should look like.

---

[23] I bet you could come up with some other things to call it!

I suppose my journey to discover God's calling began before I was even aware there was a journey to be taken. Once I was aware of it, though, few things seemed simple. So I took the best first step I could think of.

I talked to my wife.[24]

The conversation happened a long time ago, and I didn't take notes, but the spirit was this:

Her: What happens if our financial decisions become so filled with luxury and privilege that we just get *used* to it? What happens if we only want to hang out with people who live at the same level as us? What will others think of us then—and what will we think of them?

[long pause]

Me: So ... you're telling me that we're not going to the other three hotels?

My wife's answer was entirely consistent with a woman who had grown up in different circumstances from my own. Never poor, D'Aun was also never wealthy. Solidly middle-class, solidly suburban. Easily embarrassed by excess. Those circumstances mean that when *I* want to brag that I've been to seven of the top ten hotels in the world, D'Aun cringes and hopes nobody finds out how extravagant we've been.

She explained (gently, bless her) that we did at times live at an unhealthy level of luxury.[25] She reminded me that it added complexity to our lives and engendered a sense of privilege. Like we might start to *expect* it. Like it would start to separate us from others. It reminds me of this truth: "The worst side effect of wealth is the social associations it forces on its victims, as people with big houses tend to end up socializing with other people with big houses."[26]

---

[24] I know, I'm supposed to say that my first step was to fall on my knees in prayer. But let's get real. Most of us talk to the people we love and who love us. We search for honest feedback and clarity. And you know what? I believe that when we do that, we often *are* hearing from God.

[25] Which she's still doing, thank God.

[26] *Antifragile* by Nassim Nicholas Taleb

Did I want to be that kind of person? That was easy to answer: nope. But as the article had made clear, and as my wife had reinforced, I was wealthy.

Which meant that if I weren't careful, the only people I'd know would be people just like me.

The Rich Young Ruler and Shane Claiborne

Mark 10 tells an interesting story about a rich man. Jesus is walking with his disciples when the guy runs up and falls onto his knees, forcing Jesus to pay attention.

"Good teacher," he pants, "what do I need to do to live forever?"[27]

Jesus, after deflecting the attention from himself and putting it back on his Father in heaven, walks the man through the answer he should already have known.

Don't murder. Don't commit adultery. Don't steal. Don't lie. Don't cheat. Honor your parents.

The man is nodding along as Jesus ticks through the list. He already knows what he's going to say before Jesus finishes. "I've kept *all* of these since I was a kid!"

Now Jesus has a choice to make. He can congratulate the man on a life well lived. Or he can love the man.

Thing with Jesus is, he always chooses love. Loving is what he does, whether we know we need it or not—and whether we want it or not.

So Jesus looks at the man and loves him. Which means he tells him the honest-to-God truth. "You're still missing one thing. Go sell everything you have and give to the poor. You'll get your treasure back

---

[27] That's the same asked by the lawyer we talked about back in chapter 2. Apparently it was a popular thing to ask Jesus. For the record, I already know how you can live forever: Jesus saves you. Rescues you, as Colossians says, from the kingdom of darkness and brings you into the kingdom of light. Only Jesus can do that.

in *heaven,*" he adds in response to the man's obvious disappointment. "And then come follow me."

This is a single moment of possibility. Jesus's love is forcing the young man to choose between his wealth and living forever. And the man leaves, sad, because what he'd been doing right his whole life turned out not to be the path he thought it was. Sad, because even though he'd asked how to live forever, he wasn't willing to hear the answer.

Am I willing? Is Jesus giving me the same answer?

It makes me think of Shane Claiborne. Some people get the impression he has the whole wealth and poverty thing figured out, at least when it comes to following Jesus. I know it sounds like I'm being flippant, but I'm not. Together with Tony Campolo, Claiborne started an organization called "Red Letter Christians" which tries to practice the words of Jesus, especially the social teaching we find in the Sermon on the Mount (Matthew 5–7). And Claiborne walks the talk to an unbelievable degree. He's followed Jesus all around the world, from Chicago to Calcutta. He's been a peacemaker in warzones. He founded a community in inner-city Philadelphia called The Simple Way. He's absolutely changing the world and building God's kingdom, and he's doing it in part by turning his back on wealth—even by global standards.[28]

So ... maybe I should become the Claiborne of California. That would absolutely take care of the Mark 10 stuff. "You're still missing one thing, though, Roy. Go sell everything you have and give to the poor. You'll get your treasure back in *heaven.* And then come follow me."

That *is* an answer. Even a seemingly easy one. My life is a wrestling match, so it would be simpler to give it all away.

But simple isn't a synonym for best or wisest.

---

[28] Claiborne has written a bunch of great books. Check them out—along with some of the projects he's working on—at www.thesimpleway.org. And definitely go hear him speak if you can.

Say I wake up tomorrow morning and decide to give it all away. Say I can somehow give all of my money to organizations and individuals who are making a tangible difference in the world, and that there are no unintended negative consequences or harm. That's impossible, by the way, but for the sake of argument, say I figure it out. I've broken the power of wealth in my life the only way that works: by giving it away. As Andy Crouch writes, "the only real antidote to the temptations of money is lavish generosity."[29] Consider the antidote administered.

I wake up the *next* morning as a cured man. And I have to admit: it feels good! Much better than the constant wrestling and reevaluating that usually describes my relationship with wealth. I eat a simple breakfast, and then I get to work.

I spend the first hour on the phone with my employees—scratch that, *former* employees—telling them they're going to have a new boss or else they'll need to find a new job. Then I begin calling my tenants, but this takes me a lot longer. I own—sorry, *used* to own—residential, commercial, and light industrial properties in a 150-mile radius. I notify everyone to expect some changes, some of which will undoubtedly be for the worse, since I consider myself to be a fair boss and a just landlord.

As the day ends, I sneak in a call to my accountant and my financial advisor. They'll survive without my portfolio, of course, but will the client who replaces me ask them to make ethical decisions like I used to?

You tell me: would those (direct) dozens and (indirect) thousands of people affected be better off? Some might counter that *different* lives would be better off if I gave everything away. That might be true, though it's setting a hypothetical good against an actual, known good.

And what about me? Would those relationships in my life be replaced with relationships that are as holy, or more holy?

---

[29] *Culture Making*, page 212.

So the wrestling continues.

It wouldn't even solve the issue to give away *more* or *most* of my money. I recently heard about a woman who, after a long and success-ful career, is now extremely wealthy. (Not 1 percent wealthy—more like 0.001 percent.) Motivated by the desire to be responsible and wise, she made some significant financial decisions. She wanted to provide for the various people and causes she cares deeply about, so she set aside basically all of her net worth into various categories: trust fund for her kids, retirement account for herself, an endowed family foundation for long-term charitable investments, a certain amount for her church and spontaneous giving, and so on.

Why do I tell you this? Because just like giving away *all* my wealth would be simpler than the constant wrestling I do, so would following the example of this woman. It sounds so simple.

But I think it would be a copout. As tempting as a one-and-done solution is, I think I'm *supposed* to wrestle with my wealth. With giving and saving and earning and investing and spending. Not just once, but continually.

The woman I heard about? I'm sure she *did* wrestle with those financial decisions. They were massive, after all, and she wanted to do the right thing. But that one-time grappling had an unexpected consequence: practically speaking, she is no longer able to change course, even if she wants to. Or ought to. Unraveling an eight-figure trust fund? Good luck with that. A wise decision can become a bar-rier to responding to God in the future if it allows us to file and forget an entire category of discipleship and obedience. This woman wrestled with her decision, but only once—and then she was fin-ished thinking about her wealth for the rest of her life. Probably for decades! That's simple, and comfortable, but how can that be a good model for living?

Life isn't static. And just as we change and grow (and sometimes regress), the world around us also changes. What other people need changes. What's best for building the kingdom changes. We may be called to a different job, a different city or country, a different church. We may be called to spend or invest our money in different ways. In my experience, we can't predict these changes. They surprise us, but they also give us the opportunity to respond in faith.

Which is why we need to stay on our toes, ready to move in whatever direction is needed.

God wants his followers to be open to change—to go where the Spirit is blowing—and to rely on him during those changes. Jesus says that he's the grapevine, and we're the branches, so apart from him we can bear no fruit.[30] Love, joy, peace, patience, and all the rest are called the fruit of the Spirit because they don't grow in our lives without God's Spirit.[31]

Put bluntly, it isn't "the fruit of sound financial planning" or "the fruit of mindlessly embracing the American dream."

I keep thinking about that story in Mark. Jesus "looked" at the man before he "loved" him. Or maybe it's better to say that looking and loving were necessarily connected. Love is always individual because love is always personal. We can't love when we're objectifying. We can dispense good advice, sure, or generally helpful principles. But we can't love unless we're loving a *person*.

God's the only one who can love the whole world successfully. All we can do is love the people in our lives. Who are the people already in my life? Who *could* be in my life? Who will enter my life in the future, and how will I respond to those unforeseen kingdom relationships? And what does my wealth have to do with it all?

Those are the questions that drive me to my knees.

Jesus didn't tell everyone he met to sell everything. It wasn't a blanket command. He said it to some, yes, but not to others—even

---

[30] John 15:5
[31] Galatians 5:22

others who were wealthy. If it's a possibility that Jesus is asking me to give it all away, then it's also a possibility that he isn't.[32]

What scares me is that if I "solve" the problem of my wealth—all at once, once and for all—*I will no longer have to consistently and persistently trust God for guidance and wisdom about my money.*

Do We Need God?

I'll never forget one beautiful sunny day at home when I was driving down the highway without a care in the world. Sure, I had things to do and take care of, but it was all normal stuff, stuff in my wheelhouse, and it didn't concern me at all. Everything in life was just clicking. Goble Properties was humming along, the kids were happy, D'Aun was happy. We enjoyed our church. We enjoyed our friends and our hobbies. There were no major worries in my life. Everything was good. I didn't even have to be anywhere by a certain time.

I'm so blessed, I thought. *I'm relaxed, comfortable, happy, content ...*

The road kept rolling past. And then I thought something else. *Life is so good, it's almost like I don't even need God.*

Instantly it felt like my soul was being squeezed by a terrible fist. Like I couldn't breathe. My heart rate shot through the roof. Right away I pulled over onto the shoulder and braked to a stop. Cars zipped past. I gripped the steering wheel tightly with both hands, motionless, because all the drama was happening inside of my heart.

What on earth was I thinking? I was a follower of Jesus. I loved Jesus. So of course I needed God. Yet there it was inside me: the ugly truth that I was content without God.

The line of thought was all too easy to follow.

---

[32] *Hey, this is Shane Claiborne. Roy gave me this book to read, and it's true: God doesn't call everyone to sell everything and move to the inner city or some foreign country. Or even to have dreadlocks like I do. For the record, I don't think God is calling Roy to sell his business and give everything away. But that's not to say he won't someday. Careful, Roy!*

My unexamined life was very enjoyable.

Growing closer to God would complicate things.

Which is why I was—as I now realized—subconsciously ignoring God.

Because if I started truly following God, my comfortable little bubble would go pop.

Was I simply being prideful? Selfish? Stupid? It wouldn't be the first time in my life. That wasn't what was causing fear to make my heart palpitate, though. What really scared me was that it just made good sense. I knew God wanted all of me. Wanted me to love him and serve him with all my heart, soul, strength, and mind. And I knew that kind of orientation meant I needed to be available for God to use.

But doing that would make my life a lot harder. More filled with uncertainty and discomfort. What could I possibly expect in return that would be better than what I already had?

Eventually I took a breath and merged back into the traffic. I wish I could say I arrived home a changed man—that it was one of those "come to Jesus" moments where I humbled myself before God, repented, and never looked back. But it wasn't like that. It took me days to organize and process my thoughts. Weeks to actually under-stand what was at stake. Eventually I managed to ask for forgiveness. (That required knowing what needed forgiving: my independence. That's a tough one for people like me.)

But at first I didn't want to. What I *wanted* was to stay comfort-able and to keep avoiding God.

We like to say that God can use anyone. That's true—but it helps if you're not completely self-sufficient and satisfied without him.

I can only tell my story in this book. Your mileage may vary. It's quite possible for the same thought—*I don't need God*—to wash through your mind without swamping you. But the more I've thought about this, the more I've come to believe that it represents a unique temptation to the wealthy.

For all the similarities I've drawn between the rich and the poor, there is this difference: the poor cannot face the temptation of a contented life without God. They face plenty of other temptations, to be sure, including many ways of forgetting God! But one option that is unavailable to them is to replace the provision and security and comfort God provides with the provision and security and comfort wealth provides.

The wealthy, though? We can work and distract and numb and insure and entertain and protect ourselves quite well, thank you very much. So well, in fact, that we can wake up one day and realize we don't need God. Not now, not ever. Our lives can be so comfortable, so secure, that we can scarcely even imagine *heaven* improving on anything. And *this* life? We've got it taken care of. We're in control.

The sinister thing is that this *works*.

But only until it stops working.

Because we're not really in control of much at all. Something always shatters the illusion.

You'll never guess what happened within the next year after my side-of-the-highway realization. My dad died. My sister died. My mom went blind. And the first cracks of the Great Recession began to splay across our business.[33]

And so I understood clearly that I *did* need God after all—and that needing God might be the first step to God using me.

Welcome to the World of Wealth

"I just want to simplify, you know? Downsize things a bit. Get back to what matters."

When was the last time you heard someone say something similar? Chances are, it was recently. I hear things like this all the time. I've said things like this.

---

[33] If you're expecting me to discuss whether God "caused" those things in order to teach me or change me, you're reading the wrong book.

It's not a bad impulse. It usually stems from the motivation to create some margin in our lives. Margin we can use to give more, or pray more, or rest more. Like Lent, downsizing can be a way to refocus (or at least *attempt* to refocus) on what is truly important.

After all, vanishingly few of us live a life of willfully competitive consumerism. If you are downright proud of your excess and materialism, you're in the minority. Most of us have too much good sense—or a strong enough sense of shame—to revel in luxury.

We're still bombarded by the temptations of wealth, however, from a pitch to buy the latest gadget to a reminder to put aside more in our retirement plan. (Even "sound financial planning" can become a selfish addiction.)

These temptations are not only temporal, though of course they are that. They are also spiritual, because each has the potential to limit our engagement with the world and increase our insularity. Over time—over the course of a thousand seemingly small decisions, perhaps—we find ourselves separated from the poor, the oppressed, and the weak. In other words, we only socialize with other people with big houses.

This is not necessarily because we don't care or because we are intentionally being selfish. More often than not, it is because we simply forget them. It's all too easy for me, whether I'm sitting in Singapore's Raffles Hotel or driving down the highway in California.

And again, I'm using my own life to talk about these issues, but I'm not talking only about people who are in the same income bracket as me. This stuff is for almost everyone in the developed world. Wealth isn't really about how much we make. Making $32,000 a year in Manhattan is quite different from making $32,000 a year in Fayetteville, Arkansas, and both are *radically* different from making $32,000 a year in Haiti.[34]

---

[34] Remember the Occupy Wall Street movement, where the "99 percent" protested against the "1 percent"? Whatever you think about their aims, *the majority of them were in the global 1 percent.* We must always train and retrain ourselves to remember that we are global citizens and that God so loved the *world*, not just Americans.

Think about wealth by asking the following questions:

Do you wonder where your next meal is coming from?

If you are in a serious car accident, will an EMT arrive to try to save your life?

Did you ever attend a free public school?

Have you ever had a job in an air-conditioned office?

Have you ever taken a vacation of any length?

Have you ever traveled more than a few hours from your place of birth?

Welcome to the world of wealth. Now all you have to do is figure out what to do with it all.

If you want to avoid evaluating your wealth, one solution is to avoid thinking of yourself as rich. The reality is, however, that criticizing the rich means criticizing yourself. Almost all of us are in this together, whether we like it or not. As one wag put it, income disparity in Western countries means talking about the haves and the have-yachts. Very few of us reading this book are actually have-*nots*

To one person, it seems excessive to belong to ten different country clubs—and there are people who belong to a lot more clubs than that. Scandalous! To others, however, belonging to even *one* country club is sinfully excessive. There's a perfectly good municipal course just down the road. To still others, a single round of golf is an act of wasteful privilege. And in this list of hypothetical people, we covered what … a couple billion? To the other several billion people on our planet, golf doesn't even exist.

Do I sound defensive with all this "what is wealth" talk? With the way I'm trying to get more people to see themselves as wealthy? Maybe. But I don't believe I'm self-justifying. I truly don't. I've spent decades wrestling with this stuff. Praying, thinking, picking the brains of people who are a lot smarter than me, hanging out with people who are different from me.

We humans are great at deceiving ourselves though, right? So I have to take the possibility of self-deception seriously. I may be engaging in a massive attempt at propping up my own assumptions. Again, I don't believe I am, because writing and speaking about (and living!) this stuff is a lot more work than just sitting back and enjoying my comfortable lifestyle.

And the *reason* I'm wrestling with this stuff is that the thought of living without God freaks me out—and because every time I begin a friendship with someone different from me, I feel like I'm getting a glimpse of the kingdom of heaven.

Swimming Pool in a Shot Glass

When you realize you don't need God, what comes next?

Either complacency or challenge.

The first choice is the easy one. Remain complacent about your wallet and your spirit—that's the model most people in the developed world follow.

And it's a huge mistake. Complete nonsense.

Whether rich or poor or anything in between, complacency is a terrible model for human life. Complacent companies stagnate or fail. Complacent animals lose territory. Complacent students learn a few things by rote, only to soon forget them.

Trouble is, complacency is so damn easy.

I'm reminded of the complex picture Jesus paints of how our allegiances work. In Mark 9:40, he says, "Whoever is not against us is for us," and in Matthew 12:30 he says that whoever is not with him is against him. Complacency is like that. If we aren't actively fighting it, we're probably living it—or at least allowing it, even if unintentionally. We can't respond to the challenges of a changing world by just relaxing and going with the flow. Engaging the challenges and actively battling complacency is difficult. It's tiring and frustrating. It's the rich young ruler choosing to take Jesus at his word and to start living a new and better way.

A friend once said to me, "You know, you can *make* yourself need God more."

Is that one of the most uncomfortable sentences you've ever read? I know it is for me. Because as soon as we hear it, we know in our hearts it is true. We *can* make ourselves need God more. The list of ways is endless. We need God whenever we do something that requires his Spirit to help us. Like loving someone hard to love, or being joyful in the midst of trials.[35]

It doesn't take a PhD in philosophy to connect the dots:

If I am a Christian, I should want to need God more.

Doing certain things will make me need God more.

So I will do these things.

If it's so simple, though, why don't I do that? Because that stuff doesn't come naturally. It's beyond uncomfortable. Which takes us to the verses that immediately follow the story of the rich young ruler I retold earlier.

The man has left, saddened and probably hopeless, because he can't imagine giving up his wealth. Remember how Jesus looked at the young man and loved him? After the man leaves, Jesus turns to look at his disciples. Loving *them* means telling them the truth as well. They must look stunned—*Wait, this guy did everything right, and now you're asking him to become poor?*—because Jesus starts by confirming that they aren't crazy. "It's true—it's incredibly hard for a rich person to enter the kingdom of heaven."[36]

Then, as they're nodding, he lowers the boom. "Fact is, it's easier to fit your swimming pool into a shot glass."

Picture the disciples' minds exploding.

---

[35] For a complete list of things we need the Spirit's help with, check out Galatians 5:22-23.

[36] If you know what "the kingdom of heaven" really means, can you let the rest of us know? Is it heaven, for eternity? Is it now, as the power of Jesus enters the world? Is it internal? Is it some combination of all these things? We'll revisit this in chapter 6.

If that were the end of the story, you probably wouldn't be reading this book. But there are some verses that follow, and they change everything.

Most of the disciples are still scooping up their brains off the dirt road, but one of them manages to call Jesus out.

"You're basically saying people with money can't be saved!"

Know what happens next? Jesus does what he *always* does: he loves. He looks at his disciples and considers who they are. He's probably glad that they're picking up what he's putting down, because that didn't always happen. He'd told them plenty of shocking things before that failed to shock, because the surprise couldn't penetrate their thick skulls. Or maybe their hearts.

This time they get it, though, and they immediately ask for help. So he looks, he loves, and he tells them the truth.

"If it were up to humans, you'd be right: no one with money would be saved. But humans don't have the last word. God's power does—and that makes even this possible."

* * *

So here I am, in California, wrestling with the rich young ruler. Trying to understand the ripples of God's commission. Trying, with the power of God's Holy Spirit, to be a witness in Thailand and Singapore …

…, and in Belize and Haiti …

… and in the Bay Area and in Silicon Valley …

… and at home.

It's the farthest thing from easy. It isn't natural. Wealth has great potential, yes, but remember what *potential* means: the capacity to become something in the future. Wealth can become something of God or something not of God. It can build and it can raze.

How can I be saved? How can I need God more? How can I be the sort of person God uses?

I'm the guy who wanted to stay at every single one of the best hotels in the world. The guy who grew up in a junkyard and was happy to leave it behind. What I know is that on my own, I'm trying to fit a swimming pool into a shot glass.

That's how the Goble paraphrase renders the tension in Mark 10:25, anyway. The NIV puts it like this: "How hard it is to enter the kingdom of God! It is easier for a camel to go through the eye of a needle than for someone who is rich to enter the kingdom of God."

This is why God had better show up, and why I'd better be watching—because without him, this whole project is impossible. Without God's help, I *can't* follow Jesus.

The life of a rich person following Jesus is a life of bashing and bumbling into exasperating, unwinnable situations, time after time after time. It's a hopeless life unless God intervenes.

It's choosing to be a bruised, beat-up camel.

~5~

THE HEART OF IT ALL

This whole thing sucks.

Following Jesus as a wealthy person is a pain in the ass. And a pain in the conscience, the soul.

The Bible seems to say one thing, the church another. Culture one thing, my heart another. Each day can feel like a wrestling match. I worked hard to get *out* of the junkyard ... and now it's pulling me back in? There's got to be an answer. A way out.

Many in my position take the path of least resistance. Rather than wrestling, they call uncle and tap out. Wealth wins. Comfort and self-sufficiency and pride win. The lie that prosperity is God's sign of approval becomes more and more believable.

I may be a slow learner, but I know that's wrong.

Hence the allure of a true alternative. Of giving all my wealth away and living a life of holy simplicity. Becoming a modern-day saint. *Isn't he the one who gave away everything? I could never do that. God must really be using him in a powerful way.*

Yet have I been given these incredible gifts—education, parental involvement, societal privilege, a thriving business—for the sole purpose of sacrificing them? I make a grand gesture ... and then what? I become a modern-day fool. *Isn't he the one who gave away everything? I'd say he's an idiot. God had kingdom plans for that wealth, and Goble chucked it all out the window because he couldn't handle the pressure.*

God so loved the world, while I'm commanded not to. Money is evil and money is capable of great good.

I'm beyond confused.

I'm right there with the disciples, staring incredulously at Jesus. I love him, and I've been following him for most of my life, but some of the things he says still shock me. Some clear-cut answers would absolutely be welcome. A step-by-step guide, direct from God, detailing exactly what people like me are supposed to do with what they've been given.

With wealth.

With the call to remember the poor.

With God's grace and gifts.

I've been chasing that kind of clarity for decades. I've chased it all the way to the other side of the world and back again. I've hunted for it inside Scripture and inside my own heart.

I'm pretty sure it doesn't exist.

Did I mention this sucks?

* * *

But what if it's supposed to suck?

What if the whole point of what I've been given is the creation of something unexpected and joyful? What if building the kingdom is far more complicated than choosing between crude extremes? What if the difficulty is part of the way we avoid complacency?

What if a junkyard isn't a collection of rusted cars, but rather a collection of rusted ideas, hopes, and possibilities? What if the things we long for are actually waiting, covered in rust—waiting to be discovered and used? What if a junkyard isn't one specific place, but a type of brokenness inside all of us and in our world? What if the junkyard is the place redemption always begins? What if God's kingdom isn't built from scratch, ex nihilo, but rather is recreated and redeemed out of every broken but beautiful life?

What if there is an alternative to forgetting the poor, just as there is an alternative to embracing excess?

What would a life like that look like?

What if there's not a single answer to that question, but rather a lifetime of possibilities?

What if following Jesus looks less like a one-time prayer and more like a lifetime of wrestling?

And what if the only way to answer such questions of the heart is to keep asking them?

~6~

THIRD RIPPLE: CALIFORNIA

"Have you been to Old School Cafe, that new supper club?" It wasn't the first time I'd heard the question. I hesitated, only to be asked a follow-up question.

"But you *know* about it, right?"

Normally I'm fine with being a bit out of the loop, but this had gone on too long. It was time to pay attention to this new restaurant. When I did, I discovered it was Old *Skool* Cafe, and it was ridiculously cool. Just not for the same reasons most cool restaurants are cool.

Remember in chapter 3 when we talked about Samaria? It was a place the disciples were taught to fear, which made the parable of the Good Samaritan that much more challenging for them.

And for us. Because no matter where we live, we have our own "Samaria." Perhaps it is a place we were taught to fear, and perhaps it is simply our ignorance or prejudice or cultural stereotypes that create the fear. Whatever the cause of our reluctance to help, though, Jesus calls us to conquer it.

So what does a modern-day Good Samaritan look like? I learned the answer as I got to know Teresa Goines, the mastermind behind Old Skool. She decided to serve the youth in one of the toughest urban neighborhoods of a major American city. When she did, she began to discover story after story of hope and redemption. Which is what tends to happen when Good Samaritans roll up their sleeves and get to work.

Old Skool Cafe transports patrons back to Harlem's pre-war Jazz Age. From the waitstaff's black suits and red fedoras to the live music, from the classy chandeliers to dishes inspired by African-American cooking, the experience is like being warped back to a more gracious time. You've got to look below the surface, though, to discover what makes this place really different. Old Skool has a specific mission that most businesses don't: to give a lifeline to struggling kids[37] in urban San Francisco. It's a faith-based violence prevention and life skills program that provides jobs and job training by way of a 1940s style supper club. Youth are employed at every level of the business, from the kitchen to the waitstaff to the managers and purchasers. Anyone can give a job, but these kids are being given a new way of life.[38]

The kids won't stay at Old Skool forever. That isn't the vision. The vision is to give them a way to *live*. For the next week, the next year, the next fifty years. Basically, Old Skool takes kids who are—statistically at least—a lock for future trouble and puts them inside a web of support: mentorship, accountability, peer modeling, and employable skills.

The result isn't just changed lives. It's saved lives.

I learned all this when I was invited to speak at a Bay Area event for my alma mater, along with Teresa, an alumna from the same college. (I think the theme must have been "Beauty and the Beast.") D'Aun and I were seated with Teresa (making it *two* beauties and a beast), and both of us were struck by her vision and passion.

As Teresa says, her job can be summed up as bringing hope to a neglected generation. Practical hope. It reminds me of a section in the book of James that talks about faith and works. If someone has a practical need we can meet, James says, but all we do is wish them well

---

[37] At risk, previously incarcerated, and foster care kids.
[38] That was mostly a nice bit of rhetoric. Because the reality is that *not* everyone can give a job to kids like this. This is partly because of our employment rules that require disclosure of things like felony convictions and partly because not every employer *wants* to give kids like this a chance.

in the name of God, what good is that? If we're going to talk about God, we need to act like God would act.[39]

It's not easy to get a job at Old Skool. Youth applicants have to submit letters of recommendation, be interviewed, craft a personal essay, and—if accepted—submit to a months-long training program. They learn about how to manage their finances and apply for other jobs. They make short- and long-term goals and meet with mentors who will help keep them on track. They work on their GED if they don't have a high school diploma. And they agree to strict requirements for timeliness and behavior.

At the end of the day, though, Old Skool Cafe is a taste of heaven. It's how things are supposed to work: transformed people transforming others. Dozens of lives per year, each of whom touches countless others. Each of whom hopefully *changes* countless others. And they will be witnesses to hope in San Francisco, all over California and the rest of the country, and even across the world.

Sound familiar?

Bags of Money

In the last section, I said that Old Skool is a taste of heaven. That's a phrase you hear quite a bit, even outside churchy circles, and it usually means something relatively banal, equivalent to *really great*. But I want to think about it in a more literal sense. What is the kingdom of heaven actually like—and can we taste it in this life?

That's a question Jesus found himself speaking to often. Not *answering*, exactly. But Jesus certainly told quite a few stories about the kingdom of heaven, and the gospel writers sometimes wrote them out together, as if they knew readers would simultaneously be fascinated and continually confused. Something inside all of us wants to be in the kingdom of heaven, but none of us quite knows what that means.

---

[39] If in doubt, act like Jesus.

In Matthew 25 we find one of the most interesting of Jesus's "here's what the kingdom of heaven is like" stories.

So there's this guy, riffs Jesus, warming up to his story, who's going on a journey. He's wealthy, so before he leaves he calls together his servants and gives each different amounts of money, according to their abilities. He's got a sense already for who he can trust with what, but this will give the servants a chance to either prove their master wrong or confirm his assumptions.

While he's gone, the servants take different approaches to his money. The one who is given the most money immediately goes and "puts his money to work." The one who is given a bit less money does the same, while the one who is given the least takes the money and stuffs it under his mattress where it will be safe.

It takes a long time, but eventually the wealthy man returns. The first thing on his agenda is settling accounts with his servants. Now that he's back, the money he entrusted them with is once again his. (It was his all along, of course, but his servants were acting as stewards in his absence.)

The first servant reports that by putting his money to work, he was able to double it. Then he waits to see what his master says. He probably breathes a huge sigh of relief when he hears, "Excellent work! You've proved that you're my kind of leader, so I'm going to put you in charge of even more. Let's celebrate!"

At that point, the second servant steps right up. He gets the same treatment as the first. Things are going well.

Except there's still the last servant. This is the guy the wealthy man didn't trust with much: only 20 percent of what he'd given the first servant.

"I was afraid of losing your money," the third servant reports, "since I know how demanding you are. So I hid it, and look—I've still got all of it."

But his statement rises into a question at the end, because he can already tell from his master's face that he made the wrong call when he hid the money.

The master shakes his head. "So you *knew* how demanding I am ... but you figured that didn't apply to you? You could have at least put my money in a bank and drawn some interest on it while still protecting your skin!"

Then the master turns to the first servant. "His money is yours, since you know what to do with it. You've got a knack for creating wealth, and together we're going to create even more."

Then the master turns to the third servant one last time. "And you? You're done working for me, starting now. Even the little responsibility I gave you turned out to be too much."

End scene—and return to our topic.

As we look at this parable, a few things stand out. First, the plain subject is wealth creation. Second, the plain message is that when your master entrusts you with wealth, your aim should be to grow that wealth.

Does that sound uncomfortable? Does it sound *wrong*?

There are so many mixed messages about wealth—as we'll explore further in a few pages—that there's a good chance we've heard this parable not so much *explained* as explained *away*.[40] The bags of money aren't *really* money, according to some. Rather, they represent our talents or gifts. As if our talents and gifts don't include wealth creation and wealth!

Now I'm not saying the bags of money can't speak to us about many aspects of what it means to follow Jesus and to work toward the kingdom of heaven. But I'm *also* saying that we're looking at a clear teaching about *money*. And Jesus, the storyteller, wants us to see that creating money and increasing money aren't bad things.

---

[40] It's the same thing that happens with certain straightlaced interpreters of Song of Solomon. When the groom says things like, "Your lips drip nectar, my bride," these commentators get a bit uncomfortable, and skip right past the plain—and erotic—meaning. It must be about ... um ... the church! It can't really be about kissing, right?!

In fact, we could say that we are commanded to create wealth. The only guy in the story who gets in trouble is the one who runs away from money.

There's just one catch: our aims in wealth creation must align with the Master's.

Check Your Alignment

That's a seriously big "if"—creating wealth is good, *if* our aims align with God's aims.

But I'm pleased to report that I've got it all figured out. I've discovered the solution. And once I share that solution with you, you can mindlessly copy what I do and keep making money hand over fist!

Yeah, right.

I'm spreading the manure a bit thick here. For effect—and maybe to relieve the tension. Because the "if" we're dealing with *is* massive. Wealth creation is good—commanded even—if our aims align with God. But the trouble with aim is that even a little difference makes a *huge* difference.

Imagine you're flying to Hawaii from Los Angeles. That's 2,500 miles. If your heading is off by only a few degrees, you're going to miss Hawaii by dozens or even hundreds of miles.

A tiny variation in aim can cause us to miss the target, which is why I've tried to put in place some practices—I could also call them disciplines, or reminders—that help keep my aim true. These aren't surefire ways to solve every problem of wealth. They don't make me perfect. In fact, I practice them because of how imperfect I am. These are simply ways to help me stay healthy and balanced in the ongoing wrestling match of life.

They are:

Viciously attack ego

Shut up and listen

Value community

I need these practices because the wrestling match never ends. Temptation never ends. If I try to live my life *constantly* grappling with God about what is right, what is best, what is fair—every hour of every day, in every decision—I'm going to be perpetually exhausted. I'll eventually give up and seek a safe compromise solution, which, in a way, is to lose the wrestling match with wealth, allowing it to manage me rather than the other way around.

These three practices help me manage the tension. They're compass checks to keep me on course. And without further preamble, I'm going to tell you a bit more about each one—usually by way of how I've failed at each one. Because I'm writing this, it will inevitably sound like I have it all figured out. But I don't. These are live issues for me.

Okay, let's get to it. Specifically to the story of how starting to partner with Teresa and Old Skool helped me correct my aim.

Viciously Attack Ego

After I got to know Teresa, there came a point when she asked me to join a team that would take Old Skool to the next level. Supportive of her mission, I asked her what the plan involved.

Her answer was simple. "Buying the building we're leasing."

I think I made some sort of noncommittal noise. Maybe I managed a thin smile. But my mind was already cranking on all the ways her idea was a bad idea.

See, she had come to me with her "good" idea, but I had an even *better* idea: she should listen to me and forget about her current idea. I knew more than she did. I was experienced and smart, logical and cool-headed. She was a dreamer, and that was good in certain circumstances. Now we were talking real estate, though, and I was in my element. So I thought through my key objections. The Cafe was currently in an ideal neighborhood for its mission—which meant a bad neighborhood which wasn't *that* bad. But that area of the city was gentrifying, so would the location still be good in five years, or ten? And Old Skool did not have a large budget, so buying the property might mean biting off more than they could chew. Not to mention the small size of the building would limit expansion possibilities in the future.

I had many more questions, but those were enough to start with. I knew Teresa would trust me, the expert, and I would have a chance to pat myself on the back again. Which was when I realized it was time for another beat-down on my ego.

The reason for viciously attacking ego is simple: the more I value my own intellect, skills, experience, and so on, the more likely I am to cut everyone else out of the loop. Including God. But that's how ego is: like a hydra combined with a jack-in-the-box. It'll keep popping up, and coming back, and showing up in unexpected places. Over and over and over. So you attack ego. I have enough experience now that I can start to recognize when I'm acting like a walking, talking ego. Or more often, I'm fortunate enough to be married to D'Aun, who can—and does—point out when my ego rears its head. I also have a few key friends who love me enough to challenge me. Absent external input, you can only attack your ego *some* of the time, though, because you can only *catch* it some of the time. Giving select friends and family license to speak the truth to you is vital.

Shut Up and Listen

The best way to attack ego? That leads directly to my second practice—shut up and listen—because the primary way to deflate your own pride is get outside of your own head. But even listening more is a tricky one, mostly because it can seem like you're listening when you really aren't. I had dozens of informed questions for Teresa, for example, but I was using my questions to *tell* Teresa things. I was spouting opinions disguised as questions.

It's exceedingly difficult to listen if there's nothing you're listening *for*. When I already know all the answers, the only kind of communication that will interest me is one-way: me telling things to others.

My several hats got in the way of my ability to hear Teresa. In this case, the relevant hats were arrogant real estate expert and demanding donor. Once I took those off, I discovered something that is often true: the answers you think you know are merely assumptions—and sometimes you don't even have the right questions.

Teresa patiently walked me through the answers to each of my questions. Yes, the neighborhood was changing, but this particular area of San Francisco would be in need for a decade or more. And if it should improve, the value of the building would see a corresponding rise, which would help with any relocation. Yes, the building size was limited, but the restaurant was only open two to three nights a week, so there was room for future expansion within the existing space. And yes, the budget was a challenge, but with a successful capital campaign the mortgage payment would be less than the current rent.

Basically, she was right and I was wrong—but if I hadn't made an effort to actually listen, I never would have known that. By trying to get my ego out of the way so I could listen to and learn from someone else, I grew and changed for the better.

Value Community

This of course leads directly to the value of community. This is something that's ridiculously hard for me to grasp and practice—and if you're reading this book, there's a good chance it's hard for you as well.

I've been independent since my junkyard days. Independence was a core family value for the Gobles, something my John Wayne father instilled deep into my soul. And I didn't get any less independent as I aged. (I was going to say "matured," but …)

Remember that guy who started making mental plans to visit the three missing hotels on the top ten list? That guy was *not* into community. To this day I struggle with the desire to forge ahead alone. Even my blog uses the catchphrase, "Lead, follow, or go your own way." So when I heard that Old Skool was going to require a group—several groups—of people to get the building deal done, I sighed. Deeply. I know how committees work. We all do.

The short-term task force was going to be two things: well intentioned and ineffective. That's just how those things go.[41] I was certain that the conglomeration of folks coming together for this project would have a lot in common with Macbeth's bleak assessment of life: full of sound and fury, signifying nothing.

What unfolded was almost the opposite of what I'd predicted. Over the following weeks and months, unexpectedly good things began to happen. I met people I never would have met otherwise. I formed friendships with experts in fundraising, accounting, leasing, negotiating, and banking. We respected each other's areas of expertise while asking thoughtful, informed questions and learning. We were united in the goal, honoring to each other, and eager to serve. We made the necessary decisions and moved forward with tasks in a smooth, unified manner.

For my part—which wasn't to make egotistical pronouncements or to listen to myself talk, remember—I reviewed the leases and purchase contracts, advised Teresa on price points, and helped negotiate the loan terms.

And the whole thing worked. Seamlessly. Teresa deserves the lion's share of the credit, of course. But as she'd be the first to tell you, she couldn't have done it without her team. Without me and without every other person who participated in the vision.

I'm not saying such community doesn't happen outside of Jesus. I'm just saying it's a lot less likely.

And when a community does form because of Jesus, there's a danger it will start to change the world.

So: viciously attack ego, shut up and listen, and value community.

These aren't principles you put in place once and then forget about. They aren't foolproof. Rather, they're proof against the foolishness of overvaluing yourself, of being too quick to speak, and of operating as a lone wolf. And they might just help you—like they help me—break down the walls that separate me from others.

---

[41] Especially when it involves "ministry." Don't get me started down that road.

Turn off the Autopilot

In chapter 4, I noted that wealth has potential: to do good, to do evil, or—most likely—to do a mixture of both.

Isn't that how life works? Airplanes carry people to distant lands and also carry bombs. Every technology or idea can be used or abused. Even our gifts work this way. A charismatic communicator can lead a peaceful revolution or a cult. The key lies in the *ends* to which any *means* are applied, and in the humility to be correctable along the way.

Paul talked about exactly this in the first letter he wrote to the fledgling church in Corinth.[42] Again, brothers and sisters, let us turn to the Goble paraphrase. Here's the gist of what Paul is saying in 1 Corinthians 12:

There are many different gifts, but they're given by the same Spirit—and for the same reason! We're not talking about individual success or glory, but about the common good. The Spirit's gifts exist for the benefit of everyone. So things like wisdom, knowledge, faith, power, foresight, and discernment all exist because of God's Spirit and for the purposes of God. But as soon as we realize the wide variety of gifts, our human temptation to pride strikes. *This gift must be more important than that gift*, we think. (Guess which gifts we usually give a higher value to? Bingo—the ones *we* were given.) To counter that, think of the church as a body. We treat our bodies as unified wholes, and we instinctively know that every part of our body is important. The feet need the hands, the eyes need the brain, and so on—and even if we say that a part such as the brain is more important, the body can't be *just* a brain! Wake up to the reality that God's Spirit gives *lots* of gifts, and never forget that *every* gift is given for God's purposes.

---

[42] More than any other church Paul shepherded, Corinth gave him trouble, which is one of the reasons he had to write them two letters. The second one is a lot less patient.

You may have heard talk about these gifts before, usually in the context of church. But what I want to do is connect this passage to the gift of wealth creation.

Our churches can feel crazy when it comes to talking about wealth creation. Like, the kind of crazy associated with bat guano. On the one hand, few people blink an eye if a Christian (even from the pulpit) attacks money as evil and the wealthy as potentially evil. On the other hand, wealthy people are often especially welcomed to churches and Christian organizations.[43] It's almost like the message to the wealthy is, *You're sort of tainted ... but we could sure use your tainted donations!*

However, Paul is talking about a multitude of gifts given to us by God. His concern, it seems to me, is not to exhaustively list every possible gift, but rather to point out that *any* gift from God needs to be used for God's purposes. Looping back to Matthew 25, isn't that the same thing the master is after in the story Jesus tells? The master gives his servants money and applauds them for making more of it while he is absent.

Some of us, the Bible teaches, *are meant to create wealth.*

Sounds provocative. And it begs several important questions, but the answers to those questions take us back to the scriptural truth that wealth can be a gift.

Why are we meant to create wealth, and for whom?

Here's Paul's answer: for the building up of the church, for the good of others, and for the glory of God. In other words, our aim needs to match the Master's.

Money isn't evil. It just isn't. If someone tells you money is evil, that's their opinion and nothing else. Money is a tool. It is also a temptation. It's many things, in fact, but evil isn't one of them. The Bible never says that money is evil. The historic church never claimed money was evil.

---

[43] James 2 tells us this has been going on for two thousand years, which is both a comfort and not a comfort.

Teresa Goines doesn't think money is evil, either.

Before she started Old Skool Cafe, Teresa was a juvenile corrections officer in Southern California. You know—working with wandering kids who needed someone to show them the way home, which is also what she does now. But she noticed something about her job: it didn't reach far enough into the kids' lives. She was helping them with a moment in their lives—just before or after a run-in with the law—but she felt unable to help them with the *rest* of their lives. Even if the kids wanted to get back on the right track, the deck was stacked against them. Same old friends, same old habits. Recidivism 101.

That's how Old Skool was born. Now she can help those kids do so much more, from buying their first car to feeling positive about their lives for perhaps the first time. Money purchased Old Skool, and Old Skool saves lives. Wealth creators joined a community that developed, funded, and sustains Old Skool, and Old Skool saves lives.

Here's the beautiful part: Teresa still needs juvenile corrections officers to refer kids to her, just like she needs guys like me to help her negotiate loans. *There are many parts in the body, but they all need each other ... and every part is meant to work together for God's purposes.*

And thank God. Because if we're serving a God who can only use some of us? Then we probably aren't serving God, but rather a god we've made in our own image.

Know what Teresa wants to do next? That's an actual question, not a rhetorical one. Take a minute and think about what she might do, now that Old Skool owns a building, has graduated a cohort of kids, and managed to win one of CNN's "Heroes of the Year" awards a few years back.

The reason I ask you to predict the future of Old Skool is that it connects with Matthew 25 and 1 Corinthians 12. Teresa took her Master's gifts and "put them to work" for the common good. And she kicked butt! So what happens next? Does God's Spirit change her from an "eye" to a "foot," taking away her current set of skills and gifts and passions and replacing them with something entirely new? Or is it more likely that she'll hear what the first servant does in

Matthew 25:21: "Well done, good and faithful servant! You have been faithful with a few things; I will put you in charge of many things. Come and share your master's happiness!"

There's a good chance you won't be surprised when I tell you that Teresa wants to start Old Skool Cafes in other cities and that she wants some of the kids who have graduated from her program to help her. "The whole structure of this organization is meant for the youth to keep rising up in leadership and management. I'm a big believer in ownership," she says. "The more decision-making opportunities they have, the more life-changing it is."

Teresa is talking about wrestling! The more decisions we have to make, the more we grow. When we're young, we don't always think much about life. Either that, or we think we have it all figured out already! Maybe that's not a huge deal for a short season, but when it becomes a way of life, we're in trouble. I'm convinced that God doesn't want us to have it all figured out. God asks us to turn off the autopilot.

Why?

Because when we *don't* have it all figured out, that's when we need God and the gifts of God's Spirit.

God gives many gifts because he wants many, *many* people to flourish. To be saved.[44] From San Francisco to Singapore and from slums to five-star hotels. And the way God sees that happening is us, working together as a Body, empowered by his Spirit.

Experience tells us that sort of stuff is impossible. Just like one plus one can't equal three, we can't pull off that kind of stunt. We can't use wealth wisely. We can't resist temptation. We can't attack ego and listen and build community. Some walls are simply too high.

Just like it's impossible for a camel to fit through the eye of a needle.

---

[44] Technically I should say God wants *all* people to flourish and be saved, which is what the Bible tells us. But that idea can be scary, so I put it into a nice, safe footnote.

Impossible, that is, when it's up to us humans. That's what had the disciples so freaked out in the story we told in chapter 4.

Luckily, blessedly, providentially, it's not up to us. Ultimately, it's up to our Master, with whom all things are possible. Even a bruised camel squeezing, somehow, through the eye of a needle.

We're part of a diverse body, gifted by God's Spirit with *every* gift we need. Not just to be "saved," but to usher in the kingdom of God across the entire planet ... but beginning in our own neck of the woods. Even in our junkyards.

That's why Old Skool means so much to me, because it's so close to home. It's in the nearest ripple of my life. It teaches me that my gifts matter to God's kingdom and that I don't have to travel across time zones to follow Jesus.

Of course, that doesn't mean I can't also travel *across* time zones. Which is good, because I absolutely love Belize.

~7~

SECOND RIPPLE: BELIZE

Remember all the stories I told about Belize in chapter 3? They had something in common, and it wasn't only their location. In each case, someone—okay, usually me—was caught up in too many one-way conversations and assumptions.

We humans naturally put up walls between each other. Any pretext will do: race, gender, age, nationality, job, education, politics, income, you name it. We specialize in walls. Always have, always will. And our primary tool for building walls is thinking we know something when we don't.

I wish I could tell you "that was then, this is now." But it's not that simple.

Learning lessons from the past is definitely a good first step. But there's knowing ... and then there's doing. It's too easy to deceive ourselves into thinking knowledge and action automatically go hand in hand. "Those who forget the past are doomed to repeat it," we hear for the umpteenth time, and we nod. *Too true*, we agree, *too true*. Yet remembering the past isn't enough—we have to act.

My dad borrowed his philosophy from his alma mater: *Acta Non Verba*. He drilled into me my entire life that "action not words" was the way to operate. And he was right.[45] "Learning a lesson" isn't enough. We need to change our behavior in the present, just like we need to be open to changing it again in the future. But how?

---

[45] Dad was agreeing with the book of James, and frankly the whole of Scripture.

I've come to believe that the best solution—the best way to erase false assumptions and tear down walls and change the future—is to surround ourselves with cultural translators.

Basically, cultural translators are the bridge between knowing and doing. Like an effective language translator, a cultural translator is able to breach the walls that separate people, even when people are speaking the same language. These walls can be so simple to tear down that, at least in hindsight, it seems ridiculous that they ever stood at all. But *without* a cultural translator, even the weakest walls can continue to trip us up.

For the first few years at Jaguar Creek, whenever I'd share one of my good ideas with Tono, our head maintenance guy, he'd nod and reply carefully, "Well, we could try that." And I thought he actually meant we could try it! Of course what he really meant was, "That's the worst rich-white-guy idea I've ever heard, but I'm too polite to tell you that ... and maybe when your idea fails, you'll learn something." One time, we needed to find a solution for our perpetually leaking thatch roofs. I suggested putting a metal roof underneath them, allowing the thatch to be just decorative. Tono replied that we *could* do that. So I started to research my solution, only to quickly discover how expensive and complex it would be to implement ... which Tono knew all along. If I'd asked him for his suggestion first, he could have translated for me and explained how *my* idea would result in decorative, but rotten and moldy, roofs.

Other times the walls can be higher. I mentioned that we need cultural translators even when we both speak the same language. One of the reasons is that common language can deceive us into thinking we understand.

The apostle Paul faces this when he makes a visit to the heart of first-century philosophy and learning: Athens.[46]

---

[46] Acts 17

Something intriguing happens when he's there. He spends his days crisscrossing the city, speaking in synagogues and the marketplace, and he picks up a crowd of folks. They follow him, pulled by the gravity and light of his message. Traditional Jews, God-fearing Greeks, Epicurean philosophers, Stoic philosophers, and random folks who happen to be milling about the streets with nothing better to do.[47]

Sometime during Paul's wandering it hits him: there are *way* too many idols in this place. It's almost as if the Athenians are using idols as insurance policies. An idol to ensure a good harvest? Naturally. But what if there also needs to be an idol to ensure that the blades of the harvesters' scythes stay sharp? Go ahead and carve out a little idol for that too—what's the harm?

So Paul gets fed up, and standing in front of the leading thinkers and talkers of the city, he starts translating. (Culturally, that is.)

It's clear that you're religious—like, really religious. You have idols for everything under the sun. And this blew me away: you even have an idol inscribed with the phrase "To an Unknown God." Are you kidding me? Now you don't even know the very thing you claim to be worshiping! But I do. That "unknown" god can be known—he wants to be known in fact—and I'm going to introduce you.

Paul proceeds to tell them about the unknown God they've been missing: Jesus. (By the way, this is an example of a time it's absolutely true that "Jesus is the answer.")

Now I know some readers will object here. This is just good old-fashioned cultural imperialism. Here comes a foreigner, telling the locals what to do.

But two facts explode that assumption.

First, Paul was the underdog, not the imperialist. He was a member of a brand-new religion, hailing from a backwater region of the

---

[47] As Luke wryly notes, "All the Athenians and the foreigners who lived there spent their time doing nothing but talking about and listening to the latest ideas." Sounds like some hip coffee shops I've heard about.

empire. He was basically the crazy guy on the street corner. Second, while some of the Athenian elite sneered at what Paul was saying, others told him that they wanted him to come back and keep dialoging with them. What he was saying made sense to them—sounded like good news to them—and they wanted to hear more.

In other words, Paul was acting as a cultural translator. He figured out a way to break through walls in order to build the kingdom.

And he didn't just figure it out. He went and *did* it.

Drink and Forget Their Poverty

Even if cultural translators are important, you might be asking, what's the harm in a little cultural misunderstanding?

The harm is that even small mistakes can prevent relationships from forming or growing.

There's a young man who contacts me once a year so he can tell me about his ministry. Except it feels like he isn't really telling *me* about his ministry. Rather, he's telling my *checkbook* about the funding his ministry needs. It seems he's not relating to the person across the table, but to an object that will help solve his problems. Building a relationship isn't one person's job, of course. I share the blame. I could reach out to him more than I do. It's difficult, though, when his motivations appear (at best) confused and (at worst) manipulative.

So walls go up—and he and I need a cultural translator to break them down. Our misunderstanding is relatively small. Yes, it prevents a relationship between us, but it's not a life-and-death issue.

However, cultural misunderstandings have a way of multiplying. And even seemingly small ones can have large consequences. Remember the "Shop till you drop!" T-shirt in Haiti, and how on my flight out of the country I was seated next to the US ambassador? That was a situation that *desperately* needed a translator. He didn't understand the real issues at stake. The consequences weren't simply that one man misunderstood one situation. If he had been able to successfully breach the walls between his world (Western, modern, wealthy, powerful, top-down) and Haiti, there's no telling how much real and lasting good he could have done at that moment in history.

What I'm getting at is that we *all* need cultural translators. Every human has difficulty relating to certain people, especially when walls exist between us. And especially when those walls can result in exploitation and sin.

That's why I love Proverbs 31:4–9 in the context of cultural translation:

> *It is not for kings, Lemuel—*
> *it is not for kings to drink wine,*
> *not for rulers to crave beer,*
> *lest they drink and forget what has been decreed,*
> *and deprive all the oppressed of their rights.*
> *Let beer be for those who are perishing,*
> *wine for those who are in anguish!*
> *Let them drink and forget their poverty*
> *and remember their misery no more.*
> *Speak up for those who cannot speak for themselves,*
> *for the rights of all who are destitute.*
> *Speak up and judge fairly;*
> *defend the rights of the poor and needy.*

This passage is often cited as a warning against drunkenness, and I see that here, but let's not miss the deeper point. These verses are a warning to people of influence who are responsible for dispensing justice. We're told not to get caught up in the lavish trappings and distractions of a rich lifestyle. Why? Because we'll forget the poor.

Instead, our positions of influence ought to be used to make and enforce just laws, advocate for the voiceless, judge fairly, and defend the rights of the poor—which is another good description of cultural translation!

We wealthy have a responsibility to the poor, yes—but also an opportunity. We can offer hope. That's part of what it means when it says, "Let beer be for those who are perishing." Not that the poor ought to drown their sorrows in alcohol, but that the rulers ought to give the poor reason to celebrate. Godly leaders help the poor look forward to a future that is more just and fruitful, which makes the present better as well.

Unfortunately, many wealthy go to the poor with good intentions yet make tragic mistakes. They can blame the poor for being poor. They can think the answer to every problem is money. They can overlook the wisdom and skills the poor have. They can unintentionally create a culture of entitlement. They can judge the moral or ethical norms of a culture too harshly. The list could actually go on quite a bit longer, but this gets the point across. (And when I say "*they* can," you could substitute "Roy Goble" for almost every example.)

And it's equally true that many poor go to the wealthy with good intentions, but because they don't have a cultural translator, they make mistakes.

Which is why if the kingdom of heaven is truly meant to be "every tribe, tongue, and nation,"[48] then cultural translators are essential.

The wealthy don't want to be judged. But they might want to be challenged—and if they ever leave their comfort zone, it will be because of a challenge. The poor don't want to be judged. But they might want to be welcomed and listened to—and if they're ever listened to, they might provide solutions and resources the wealthy cannot imagine.

A cultural translator can shut down those judgments, and in the absence of judgments, relationships can form.

---

[48] Spoiler alert: it is. Which is challenging when you stop to think about it.

Unfolding Stories

I set myself the goal of creating a list of what cultural translators *do*, because otherwise this can start to sound vague.

We might agree—*okay, sure, we need cultural translators*—but fail to picture what a living, breathing cultural translator actually looks and acts like. The danger of lists, though, is that they oversimplify. In introducing the following three points I'm not trying to put a box around cultural translation, but rather to sketch some common characteristics.

First, cultural translators help us see the inherent complexity in life. Back in our first Belize ripple, I talked about how we can leave a missions trip with a smile on our faces even though we know that poverty in the place we've just been is both grinding and endemic, or that chronic unemployment, disease, teen pregnancy, or lack of health care are common and devastating. I snarked that we can label the people "over there" as so *joyful* even in the midst of their suffering. And they might *be* joyful, but only some of the time. When we remember them as *only* joyful, we objectify them, not to mention ignore their very real problems.

There's a reason we can make that kind of mistake: because we're far more comfortable seeing people as snapshots than as movies.

We know this from *actual* snapshots. Few of us keep pictures in frames unless they are idealized in some way. We love that wide smile, that perfect slant of light, that momentary expression of joy captured by the camera. We want to capture that moment—freeze it in time— so that no matter what else is happening in life, we can always go back to that one perfect instant.

Trouble comes when we treat living people like they're photographs. When we do, we can project onto them any emotion or conclusion that we want—and usually what we *want* is to feel comfortable. To put it starkly, we can look at our mental snapshot of someone halfway across the world and imagine they are happy even when they are not.

When it comes to the poor or disadvantaged in our own cities and neighborhoods, however, that kind of objectification is not an option. We *know* the people close to us are not snapshots. We know they are struggling with complicated generational problems that simply do not have easy or quick solutions. Since we can't label them as easily as we can someone halfway around the world, we choose the next easiest thing. It's far easier to stay away, physically and mentally, than to engage.

I see this all the time. I know people who want to go to Belize or Thailand with me "to help the least of these"—yet who wouldn't go *near* the rougher areas of Oakland. They'll fly five thousand miles to pour a sidewalk or paint a church, but they won't drive five miles to have dinner with a hungry single mom living in a shelter.

This is exactly why we need cultural translators, *especially* in our own communities where we think we don't need them. Cultural translators help us—challenge us—to remember that life is a series of concentric circles and each circle includes complicated, nuanced lives. As we see in Acts 1, we're called to share God's good news close to home, first, and only then to expand around the world. We will always learn more about our own culture—and do more to help our own culture—when we do it in community.

Second, because they understand the inherent complexity in life, cultural translators look for solutions that are two-way. Which is simply to say they look for *solutions*. Because *any* real solution must be two-way. Back when we built a laundry facility for Armenia Village in Belize, we weren't *solving* anything. We thought we were, but we weren't. We lacked a relationship and two-way conversation—and that one-way flow of information made it possible for a wasteful mistake to go all the way from idea to execution to eyesore.

Cultural translators, then, ensure the necessary give-and-take is in place to overcome walls. For example, nearly ten years after the failed laundry project, I returned to the same village, this time in the capacity of leading PathLight, our educational initiative. We were launching a sponsorship program for students to continue their education past eighth grade, something very few villagers had achieved. By our calculation, Armenia Village had nearly a thousand residents, of which less than five had graduated from high school.

We'd done our homework this time around, so we knew the village loved our plan to increase educational opportunities. Still, we met with the village leaders to let them know how we were partnering with the local schools. It was a courtesy visit, where we planned to ask for their advice and make sure we weren't stepping on any toes.

We met in the conference center and began with small talk about good times in the past, the weather, and so on. It was a comfortable environment—so comfortable that it didn't take long for one of the council members to ask a fairly direct question. He didn't phrase it quite this way, but it amounted to: "So what are you going to do for us?"

The old me would've promised the world. But in the intervening years, I'd been around enough wise and effective cultural translators that I was able to keep my mouth shut. (It was also good that I kept my mouth shut because both the old me *and* the current me were sarcastic, and the timing would have been perfect for a zinger about the useless laundry facility his predecessors convinced us to build the first time around.)

All eyes were on me as I collected my thoughts. "We will be good neighbors to you, just as you are good neighbors to us," I said eventually, "and good neighbors help each other."

They nodded, waiting for me to get more specific about the kind of help I had in mind.

Except I was done speaking.

When they realized that, there was a great deal of nodding and shrugging and paper shuffling and chair scooting, followed eventually by the equivalent of, "Okay ..."

Because we'd established that any projects going forward would be relational and collaborative, we'd made life both easier and harder. Harder, because we were signing up for all the uncertainty and conflict and head-butting that accompanies genuine relationships. And easier, because we knew that whatever happened, we'd be doing it together, without one party objectifying the other.

The truth is, real relationships are frightening.

If we send a check to a ministry that's working to rehabilitate drug offenders, we don't experience any fear. But entering into a relationship with a drug offender? Or someone in abject poverty who, on any given day, could lose their shelter or food or job? That's scary stuff. Relationship implies responsibility. It's not that life becomes more complex when we enter into relationship with people different than ourselves. Rather, the complexity of life is revealed to us ... and we are invited to do something about it. Life is always complicated—especially for the poor. It is wealth that provides the illusion of simplicity, because it is wealth that allows walls to be constructed that shield us from complexity.

When I am in a relationship with, say, someone who is very poor, I find myself plagued by questions.

Did they eat enough today? Did they miss work because of car trouble—and will the missed work force a choice between repairing the car and eating?

That's uncomfortable stuff that can create a reluctance to engage. The more we know about someone, the more responsibility we have to put aside our own habits and desires in order to consider what the other person needs. I understand the temptation to remain at arm's length. All I can say is that there is something better on the other side of the fear. The fear transforms into something unimaginably good. But the only way to find out is to live your way to the answer.

Finally, cultural translators take the long view. They must, because very little happens in the short term that is lasting. Life is an unfolding story. We can't see every conclusion. We can't even *imagine* most possible conclusions. We can't predict or control the outcome of a person's story. All we can do is attempt to build healthy, holy relationships in the present.

The best way of illustrating this is a story about Pastor Carol Houston.

Carol made her first trip to Belize back in 2008, when she was trying to figure out if God might have a role for her to play there.[49]

The night she arrived, all the students and staff and visitors at Jaguar Creek gathered for dinner. We were standing in a wide circle, holding hands so we could say a prayer before eating. Just before the prayer began I noticed four boys in the corner. They were dressed like the Belizean version of wannabe tough guys. Backwards hats, jeans sagged way too low, a walk that was more like a slouch.

Carol saw them too. She quietly walked up behind them and leaned down to whisper something to them. I don't know what she said, but it was enough to make those boys yank off their baseball caps like they were on fire! She's old-school like that.

Then we prayed and the circle broke up. Everyone went through the buffet line, then found tables where they could sit and chat.

Everyone except the four boys, who had no interest in talking to anyone else. They were thinking one thing and one thing only: free dinner. They found the table farthest from everything else, took seats with their backs facing the group, then tried to look surly and threatening. And they actually *did* look intimidating. They wouldn't have *frightened* anyone, but everyone else was going to be happy to leave them alone, which was exactly what they wanted.

I wasn't the least bit surprised, though, when I saw Carol get her tray and then sit down right next to the boys. I quickly made sure I was in hearing range.

"So," Carol asked, "which one of you gets into the most trouble?" That's the kind of lighthearted icebreaker she likes.

Well, the first three kids all pointed at the fourth kid. Let's call him Aleck—short for *smart aleck.*

"Why do you get into trouble?" she asked Aleck.

---

[49] Now she and a team from her church lead regular spiritual retreats at Jaguar Creek for the PathLight students, and it's safe to say the students revere and adore her.

He shrugged his shoulders. All four mostly looked anywhere but at Carol.

Carol's second question was, "So who is Jesus to you?"

Aleck shrugged in an effort to push Carol away. I tried to keep my smile hidden. He had another thing coming if he thought *that* was going to be a good conversational road to go down with her. Soon I was pulled away into a different conversation, but I wondered what the outcome was going to be. If anyone could get through to the boys, perhaps it was Carol. But that was a gigantic if.

Busy with eating and other conversations, I didn't think any more about the most awkward dinner party in the universe. When I stood up to bus my dishes, though, I happened to glance that way again. The boys were all looking abashed—at least as abashed as any teenager can look—and one of them was sobbing into his hands. I couldn't resist sneaking closer.

" ... you *do* know Jesus," Carol was gently saying to one of them, "I *know* you do, just like you know he *loves you*. You may be denying it on the outside, but ..."

You'll never believe what happened next.

Nothing.

The boys and Carol finished eating. The boys put their hats on and slouched away. Carol flew back to Los Angeles. A year later, two of the boys were dropped from the program for failing their grade, one was dropped a year after that, and only one managed to complete high school.

Depressing? Maybe.

Realistic? Definitely. This is what I mean about cultural translators taking the long view. If translators like Carol only broke down walls when they *knew* they'd get instant results, then they'd *never* break down walls.

In the timeline of God's kingdom, breaking down walls is always the right thing to do, even when you can't see what's on the other side.

Faith Does

To be honest, my description of what cultural translators do is murky at best. Identifying those kind of people relies mostly on Justice Stewart's infamous definition: "I know it when I see it." I can rattle off a list of effective cultural translators a mile long because I have observed them—sometimes over the course of decades—tearing down walls between the rich and the poor, the urban and the rural, the Christian and those of other faiths.

You can probably list your own by this point in the book. They're people who are doing it right. People you admire and wish you could imitate.

And there's the rub: it's all too easy to feel defeated before we even try. There's a perception that such people are saintly superhumans. Since (we assume) we can *never* live in such a way, we shouldn't bother attempting.

It does take a unique person to be comfortable across cultures. It requires humility, a spirit of openness, and a reluctance to judge. Perhaps not everyone can be a translator. Perhaps not even everyone who reads this book can be a translator. But I am convinced that many more people can and that many more people need to. The fact that not everyone can do this doesn't mean no one can—and it certainly doesn't mean *you* can't. I'd argue the opposite, actually. If you're reading this, there's a good chance you are being called to this sort of kingdom building: to tearing down the cultural walls that prevent godly relationships and lasting solutions.

With that in mind, I've got some encouraging news for you. Rather than looking at the *what* of cultural translation, we're going to look at the *how* of it. And the good news is that the how is simple, biblical, and accessible to anyone who asks. All it takes is that classic trifecta of faith, hope, and love.

We sometimes carry around a mushy idea of what faith is, like it's this vague feeling of trust in some unknown but good outcome. I'm not sure where that idea came from, but it wasn't from the Bible. Read the eleventh chapter of Hebrews, for instance, which goes through almost the entire history of the Hebrew people in order to define faith like this: *faith makes you do stuff.* The book of James agrees. So do the Psalms. And Exodus and Numbers. And the Sermon on the Mount. And Revelation. The whole of Scripture agrees, really. Faith and action are inextricably linked.

I've got a great example of faith in action for you. A few days after my father passed away, back in 2006, I said to D'Aun, "We should start praying about the next stage of our life. I don't have to go to the office and run Goble Properties for Dad now. At least not if I choose to wind it down."

Just a few days later, Gordon Aeschliman, president of Target Earth,[50] called me. Target Earth was shifting, and Belize wasn't in their plans. Did I want it? I agreed to pray and talk to D'Aun.

D'Aun's first question went to the heart of the matter. "Who would run it?"

"What about Mark and Adrienne?" I wondered. They were our longtime friends, and I knew they were currently working as teachers in Costa Rica—but that was after successful careers in Silicon Valley. At the time they'd left California, they had no *reason* to go to Costa Rica, per se. Their kids were grown and out of the house, and they loved their community and church. But they felt like God was calling them to go, so they moved to Costa Rica for a year.

Initially I didn't do anything more than wonder and pray. It seemed like they'd be perfect to help us in Belize, but I expected they'd wrap up their commitment in Central America and head back to the States.

A few days later I got an unexpected message from Mark. He wanted me to pray for him and Adrienne. They loved Costa Rica, but they felt like God was "up to something." They just didn't know what.

---

[50] One of the first faith-based environmental organizations.

A few of us got together to gang up on (I mean *convince*) Mark and Adrienne to come helm a new, post-Target Earth organization in Belize, at Jaguar Creek. At the time we called it ONNA,[51] but with the aid of several bottles of wine, we came up with a better name: PathLight.

Like Dad taught me in the junkyard—though neither of us would have used these words at the time—faith is deciding to act and then watching God show up.

My friend Bob Goff says that "love does," but it's also true that *faith* does. Mark and Adrienne's faith led them to do something most of us will *never* do: move to another country for an entire year because they knew Jesus was asking them to.

What's even more challenging (and encouraging) to me is this: that act of faith didn't get them off the hook with God ... it led them to another unexpected adventure in Belize!

If faith produces action, it's no wonder hope is vital to cultural translation. Why in the world would you start a new job in a new country with an uncertain future and lower pay (and heat, bugs, and humidity) unless you had real hope that God was calling you to it for a reason? Similarly, why in the world would you scold teenagers from another country about wearing hats at dinner and then engage them in a conversation about Jesus unless you had *hope?*

It isn't just me making the connection between faith, action, and hope, by the way. The NIV Bible labels Hebrews 11 "Faith in Action," and before we read the list of actions undertaken by faith, we read this: "Now faith is confidence in what we hope for and assurance about what we do not see. This is what the ancients were commended for."

So Carol Houston sat down at a table with some surly kids, not because she knew it would be fun, or comfortable, but because she had a confident hope.

And her hope did not disappoint her.

---

[51] As in "Oh no, not again!"

Two years after that awkward dinner, Carol is back in Belize, walking through the village of Armenia, when she hears someone yelling, "Pastor Carol, Pastor Carol!"

Here comes "Aleck," running across the street and giving Carol a bear hug, which of course she returns. They step back and she looks at him. He's taller by a few inches, and he's making a brave attempt to grow his first mustache. He looks like a kid pretending to be a man.

"Pastor Carol, I found Jesus! I know he loves me, and I know him!"

What follows is more hugging, gigantic smiles, and heartfelt prayer. It's the evidence of hope.

This is the kingdom—and the church—embodied in a brown boy and a black woman, from different countries and incredibly different lives, standing on a dirt street and gushing about someone named Jesus and how they can't imagine life without him.

Isn't that a great story? It astounds me when I think about it. It fills me with hope and with gratitude for a God who operates like that.

Which brings us to the final item in our trifecta: love.

A disclaimer up front: I'm not the guy you'd normally pick to talk about love. At a recent meeting about how to grow PathLight, we were looking at how other nonprofits build around the unique personality of their founder. Which sounded great, until one of the big-shot marketing guys quipped, "Well, yeah … but c'mon, Roy, it's not like you're warm and cuddly!" So what I'm about to say is coming from this sometimes cranky perspective—but I'm saying it because I'm convinced it's true.

You likely know all the clichés about God's love. It's big, it's wide, it's abundant, it's never-ending, it's incomprehensible, it's unconditional, and so on.[52]

---

[52] I may or may not have wanted to write, "For the most part, all of that is tripe." And I may or may not have been vetoed by my publishing team.

But for me, the key feature of God's love is its *irrationality*. Remember what Jesus says in the Sermon on the Mount: *What good is it if you love those who already love you? Even jerks do that!*

God, on the other hand, loves people who *hate* him. The Bible tells us that at the same time we were actively giving God a list of reasons *not* to love us, Jesus chose to "give his life" for us. And Jesus says that someone laying down their life for a friend is the pinnacle of love. So basically God looks at humanity and goes, *I've got a lot of enemies down there, so Jesus? Why don't you go show them how much I love them.*

That's why 1 John 4:19 makes sense: "We love because he first loved us."

It's the irrationality of God's love—perfectly loving even his enemies—that makes it possible for us to love.

Here's a quick and admittedly banal comparison. Have you ever tried to help someone with a gift of time or money only to have that person refuse? And you *knew* they needed your help? A parent offers to help a kid fold the laundry. The obviously hungry teenager refuses the food you're offering and demands money instead. Once I offered a homeless man some extra clothes and he refused, saying, "No, those won't look good on me." Think of how you feel in those situations. Frustrated, right? *I made an effort to love you, because I saw you needed help, and instead of accepting it, you're pushing me* away?

Now multiply that by a few trillion and you get a sense of what it cost Jesus to love people the way he did. The way he *does*.

That kind of love doesn't make sense.

For instance, there's this guy I know who works for one of my organizations, and he … well, let's just call him a low performer. He tries hard, I assume, but at the end of the day he seems to have accomplished very little. It drives me crazy. So how should I respond to that? If you read all the management gurus about maximizing the potential of your organization, you get rid of low performers like this guy. But that's not how Jesus responds. Jesus responds with love. It's irrational. Ridiculous even. But it's what I'm called to do. So I bite my tongue, take a deep breath, and try to love the guy for who he is. He's better for it, certainly—but so am I!

Many of the relationships I've made over the years don't make sense. There are people I've met all around the world, people I love now, and sometimes I'll be asked, "Why do you love that person?" The relationship doesn't make sense from an outside perspective.

I always give the same answer. "I have no idea!"

Because they're right: those relationships don't make a whole lot of sense. There isn't a convenient rubric to explain kingdom relationships. At the end of the day, you just can't imagine *not* having them.

Thank God.

Meet Franklin

Let me tell you one last story. Or rather, let me introduce you to Franklin. He can tell his own story far better than I can. It's a story about faith, hope, and love. About cultural translation and tearing down walls. And to be candid, it's as good an answer as any to the question, "Why do you do what you do, Roy?"

> My name is Franklin. I was born on July 24th, 1993. My biological father walked away on my mother and me. My stepfather had four children of his own and treated me differently. I would sometimes cry and wonder why my father had abandoned me like an unwanted puppy.
>
> In 2006, I was in seventh grade. My dream was to become someone important in life and I knew that it would only be possible if I could continue my education. After graduating, I did not expect what happened next: my mom and stepdad abandoned me.
>
> A month went by and they did not show up. I was sick and I did not have any food to eat. I know what it's like to wake up in the morning and have nothing to eat or go to bed with an empty stomach. I know the pain, the

suffering it causes. It's not only physical, but mental as well. My brain and my body grew so weak all I could think of was how my biological parents did not care about me.

My troubles did not end there. The rent of the house was due and I had no money. I remember that night like it was just yesterday; everything was just weighing me down and my last resort was suicide, but I didn't have the heart to go through with it, even though I couldn't bear the pain anymore.

That night I promised myself to make a stand and to do something with my life. I packed some clothes and I went everywhere searching for a job. I was twelve years old at that time, and every employer told me I was too young to be employed. I had no choice but to join the work force at a farm. My hope for an education had vanished along with my parents. My heart was full of bitterness, and I hated the whole world and myself.

However, I was given a second chance. A compassionate woman, Mrs. Lily, saw my suffering and also saw something in me that I couldn't see in myself because I was so lost in darkness. I call her my angel, because regardless of her having nothing, she offered me the security of a roof over my head and three meals every day. The opportunity to have a home once again gave me perspective in life. With the help of Mrs. Lily, I was able to see clearly once again, and not only did I see clearly, but I saw pure hope. I only needed someone to show me love, to believe in me, to push me in the right direction.

In May of 2008, I was fourteen; I applied to the PathLight Sponsorship+ Program. The following month, I received a letter of acceptance. I could not contain my joy; I was smiling and jumping with happiness. I gave God thanks, and I also thanked Mrs. Lily, my God-sent angel. Even though I was rough along the edges, I managed to make good progress, while I showed strong leadership qualities throughout high school. PathLight made me feel important. There were other students in the program that had different stories and dreams; I could see the reflection of happiness and hope in their eyes. The staff of Path-Light didn't choose me and the other students only for a scholarship; they gave us their friendship, love, and encouragement.

At this point in time I am working from Sunday to Friday; on Saturdays I attend a Tour Guiding Course. My attitude is more of a gentle lamb as opposed to a roaring lion. I learned it's not about how hard one falls, but how one manages to stand up. I also learned that if you are not loved by the people that you expect to love you, love those who are willing to share their love and support with you, regardless if they are not your flesh and bones.[53]

It's been my privilege to know Franklin for several years. Helping to inspire stories like his gets me out of bed in the morning. Speaking as someone involved with PathLight, Franklin's story is a clear win we can point to.

And speaking of wins ... here's what I didn't tell you about Carol Houston's story earlier. In the time between Carol verbally slapping "Aleck" upside the head at the dinner table and their joyful reunion two years later, here's what happened.

He dropped out of school.

He married a fellow teenager.

He had a kid.

He has no real access to health care or career advancement.

---

[53] This is a slightly abbreviated version of a letter Franklin wrote. http://www.junkyardwisdom.com/2013/12/27/must-read-story-of-the-year/

By a lot of metrics, Aleck isn't a success. He's still at risk, in a big way. And what stings is that even by the metric of PathLight, *he's a failure.* Franklin gets a thumbs up, but Aleck gets a thumbs down.

But is that the only way we can look at it? Do statistics and metrics have the last word?

I say no. There isn't a quick fix for stuff like this. There will *never* be a quick fix. Life is messy, no matter where you live it. But Aleck is following Jesus, and I don't have the slightest idea where Jesus is going to lead him. What I *do* know is that it will be good in a kingdom sense.

When it comes to "fixing" what's wrong with people, we can't rely on the junkyard way. We can't treat people as objects to be pulled apart. Rather, we need to remind ourselves that people are redeemed relationally and holistically. Relationship is the only answer—relationship fueled by faith, hope, and love. That's how God started with us, through Jesus, and it's how we must approach anyone else. Relationship that has enough faith to act, even when it's uncomfortable or frightening. Relationship that has enough hope to act, even when the end of the story is so far away that only God can see it. Relationship that is irrational enough to love.

I can say with certainty: if you tell God you want to follow and serve, you *will* be used. And what happens next will surprise you, more likely than not.

It doesn't make a whole lot of sense for me to operate in Belize. It isn't convenient to get there from the Bay Area. It's not intrinsically connected to my primary business. My church doesn't have a presence there. I'm not an expert in missions or education or development. So why in the world do I spend so much energy there?

All I can say is that God put Belize on my radar.

I had to evaluate the opportunity and ask myself, "Is this the opportunity God is putting before me?"

The answer turned out to be yes, which meant I needed to start acting. Not with a clear idea of the final goal, and not without fear and uncertainty. And not by selling everything and moving to Belize!

In the kingdom economy, it's possible to lose money on a good investment. Some good investments never deliver a financial return, but instead deliver a return on people's futures. People like Franklin, and people like Aleck. People I employ even though I don't need to from a strict business perspective.

And hopefully—remember, that's a loaded word now, not a throwaway word—those people will make a long-term difference in their families, their churches, their communities, their workplaces. Or who knows. A kid who goes through PathLight might become prime minister, and an entrepreneur who rents property from me may cure cancer. (And these are my human examples of possibility—I've got a feeling that someday, God is going to connect a series of dots that will explode my mind.)

What I know is that if I had given everything away years ago, I wouldn't have this particular set of relationships and opportunities. Just like if I had stayed comfortable in California, writing nice fat checks.

I'm connected to lives and locations outside of the walls that, by default, would insulate me.

And there is no amount of *anything* that would make me rebuild those walls, because what I have discovered on the other side is so deeply good.

~8~

FIRST RIPPLE: THAILAND AND MYANMAR

Chiang Rai, in a rural region of northern Thailand, was founded in the thirteenth century. Today, a trickle of tourists come to see the Golden Triangle, the Night Bazaar, the White Temple, and the scenic Doi Chang mountain range, though Chiang Rai is certainly not a well-known international destination. Until recently, it was a relatively sleepy provincial town, but a new highway connecting it with China brings the promise of change.

We know enough about emerging economies to predict much of what will happen in Chiang Rai. Across the globe, rural people tend to move from farms to cities when given the choice. While it may be tempting for us wealthy Westerners to romanticize agrarian life in a place like Thailand, the realities of such a life are harsh. Subsistence farmers work seven days a week, often from dawn to dusk. The labor is physically demanding and unending. There are few prospects for an improved life. While it may be difficult for us to see the appeal of moving to a place like Chiang Rai, with its crowded streets, growing crime, and extremely limited resources, it all depends on what we're comparing it to. To undocumented Burmese laborers, for example, working for less than the Thai minimum wage is preferable to village life back home.

We must make a conscious effort to look beyond our immediate context. When you grow up in a tiny hut in a tiny village in Thailand— the same village where your family has farmed for generations—sometimes the only thing you can think about is escaping. And the only place you can realistically escape *to* is the closest city. If you manage to avoid being trafficked or robbed or exploited in some other way, you may set your sights on a *big* city, like Bangkok, partly because of the promising rumors about life in the cities and partly because you are desperate.

So inevitably, Chiang Rai will continue to grow. Workers whose only option was backbreaking labor in a rice field will now be able to work in shops and hotels and restaurants. Conveniences, and especially Western goods, will be easier to obtain, along with gray- and black-market items. And the new highway is sure to bring a flood of visitors and commerce—along with things less savory. Will economic and cultural change mean that the demand for child labor increases? Will it mean more truckers and traveling businessmen looking for a good time and a growing red-light district in Chiang Rai?

Will the value of a virgin girl go up?

When wealth and poverty crash together, the fallout can be that stark and that evil. There *will* be exploitation.

Think of the shipping corridor off the coast of Somalia. On the beach are people with nothing, and those people can see unimaginable wealth sailing past, just offshore. Or think of the Mexican border towns alongside Texas and Arizona, where so-called coyotes prey on people who are desperate for a chance to give themselves and their children a better life. In *The Ruin of the Roman Empire*, James J. O'Donnell writes that "great capitals and bustling cities are all well and good, but the constructive and creative energies of humankind are often best seen among the mixtures and minglings of peoples at the margins of nations and empires."[54]

That's true, but it's equally true that the margins are where the poor and vulnerable are marginalized, and victimized, the most.

In many ways, Chiang Rai remains worlds away from Klong Toey. In Chiang Rai, a short moped ride can still take you into the countryside, where you can be among rice fields and farmers and even beasts of burden doing what they've been doing for thousands of years. Yet it is that paradoxical clash of rural and urban, naïve and worldly-wise,

---

[54] James J. O'Donnell, *The Ruin of the Roman Empire*, x.

that makes a place like Chiang Rai one of the front lines in the war against exploitation and trafficking.

Which is why I wanted to visit Chiang Rai with my daughter. Just outside the current edge of the city, near a small village, is a resource center run by the anti-trafficking organization The SOLD Project. It's housed in a simple building and offers safety and hope to children and parents alike. Kids can drop in after school and get help with their homework. They can take classes and learn to protect themselves from the risks around them. They and their parents can be educated about how to save money and plan for their financial future or how to resolve domestic conflicts at home.

Remember when Rachel said that poverty is the trafficker? Here in Thailand, the fight against trafficking *is* the fight against poverty— and every other evil that contributes to the likelihood of exploitation.

This small resource center is a remote but steadfast outpost. And it's desperately needed. The work Rachel's organization does there doesn't grab media attention or generate headlines. They've never been endorsed by a celebrity. But day in and day out—and often night in and night out—they keep up the fight. If a child is trafficked, the staff at the resource center will move heaven and earth to get that child back.

The real goal, however, is to prevent that child from being trafficked in the first place.

It's an unfortunate reality that when we hear the word *prevention*, there is a good chance it will go in one ear and out the other, leaving us with a vague impression that something good has happened. But what does prevention actually look like?

It looks like a teacher spending time with fidgety five-year-olds, helping them learn the alphabet or how to count past ten. Or like a community educator—who is also a cultural translator—explaining online safety. Prevention looks like a building contractor making sure that his subcontractors pay their laborers a living wage, ensuring they don't need to do anything illegal in order to provide for their families. It looks like doing the things our culture would consider boring—the fundamental things that reduce the likelihood of exploitation happening to begin with.

These are the kinds of relational investments that stand the best chance of preventing a child from being exploited or trafficked, because they surround the child (and the child's family) with guard-rails. Prevention isn't a straight path toward justice, as my daughter says, but rather a winding road. It is along that road—with all of its curves and hills and stops and starts—that we find out if our faith actually means what we say it means.

The Problem of Too Easy

This probably isn't the first time you've heard this kind of thing. You may already be an expert. But no matter who you are or where you're coming from, once you know about something like trafficking (or any other injustice), you experience a desire to help on some level.

All too often, though, our defense mechanisms kick in before we actually do anything to help. *The problem is too big. I can't make a difference by myself. Someone else is better equipped to help. I'll do more harm than good.* Any of those sound familiar? To me they do, because I've heard them in my own head.

But those reactions don't always prevent us from helping. Sometimes we jump right in and start helping before our defense mechanisms can give us reasons not to. There's a simple reason: it can be incredibly easy to help.

Sometimes it seems effortless to make a difference because it almost *is* effortless.

You can sit on the couch in your pajamas and use your iPad to send money to an anti-trafficking organization. If the organization is effective, they'll use your money wisely. Perhaps you're helping to pay for a staff member's salary or new tires on a vehicle used to reach remote villages. So there's a real chance that the tiny, easy action you took will make an impact. It might be that your iPad activism directly contributes, for example, to someone driving up to a seedy karaoke bar in Thailand and leaving with a recently trafficked girl, taking her back to a safe house.

I bet you can feel the "however" coming. Here it is:

Today it's easier to help solve problems than ever before. However, that very ease makes it harder to actually follow the commands of Jesus.

Take the current trendiness of anti-trafficking campaigns. I know it sounds terrible to say that—how can literally saving children from extreme evil be *trendy?* But we have to acknowledge that's part of the messy world we live in. If we look back across the decades, we can identify various causes that resonate in our collective consciousness. Famine relief. Earthquake relief. Tsunami relief.

This means there is a high likelihood that at some point, anti-trafficking will cease to be trendy. Committed people will still give their lives to that cause, certainly, but the number of folks using their iPads to donate will drop. Sermons about it will dry up. Blog posts about it will generate fewer views.

What I'm saying here could easily be labeled as cynical—especially because I'm the guy who's actually published stuff like this:

You can be part of this solution. You can join them. Go to the website, make a gift, join the cause. You might think, "But it's only a small gift, it's not enough." Phooey. What you consider a small gift is huge in this community. Even $4 a week is transforming. Do not use the excuse that your gift is too small; celebrate your gift as courageous!

Corny, eh? But here's why I bring this up: because good can be the enemy of better and best. Because sitting on our couches and tweeting something about justice might be a world away from what Jesus is calling us to do. Hell, even visiting Thailand might be a world away from what he's calling us to!

Jesus summed up all of Scripture like this: *Direct everything you have and everything you are and everything you do toward loving God and loving your neighbor.*

If all of us who follow Jesus followed him in concentric circles, rippling out across the world, making and maintaining relationships as we go, I believe there would be fewer anti-trafficking organizations … and that would be a good thing! It takes three things to start an anti-trafficking organization: a desire to help, a bit of time, and a website. And precisely because it is amazingly easy to "start something," too many things get started.

Can't Get Comfortable

Why do I say too many? Because sometimes a desire to help can best be activated in some other way. I'll be the one to point this out: if you're the student sitting in your dorm room, burning with a passion to save kids from being trafficked, *that doesn't mean you must start your own anti-trafficking organization.* It might be that the way you can be most effective is to stay in school, get a master's degree in intercultural studies or business, and become a COO for the anti-trafficking organization someone else already started.

To nuance this a bit, let me suggest a few more cranky conclusions.[55]

If you are making in the high six figures working in the tech industry, and you feel guilty, don't quit your job so that you can become a social worker or ladle soup at a shelter.

If you earn a high wage as an investment banker managing other people's money, don't assume you'll add value to the life of somebody in Klong Toey by quitting your job and offering financial advice for free.

If you support yourself as a teacher in a middle-class suburban neighborhood, don't assume God's kingdom will be stronger if you quit to serve in an underprivileged neighborhood.

If you're a student wondering why you're going into debt to finish a degree, don't assume your real calling is to drop out and serve in the "real" world where the poor live.

If you own a profitable small business and wonder if you're really making a difference in the world, don't assume God wants you to sell everything and move to Africa to drill wells.

If you're a musician, writer, actor, or any type of artist, don't assume the skills your benefactors pay you for need to be given away for free.

---

[55] I can be a grump, but I try to be an equal opportunity grump.

Now, *might* those things be true? Might you be called to these "radical" acts? Of course! But these are difficult questions with even more difficult answers. When we start living the Great Commission, there's every chance we're going to do less, but *be* better. More effective, more relevant, more like Jesus. Why? Because our actions will naturally flow out of our relationships. We'll know real people with real needs, and we'll work together to solve those needs. We'll help each other and give hope to each other.

That doesn't sound like a very inspiring plan, I know. "Start by making friends with people different than yourself. Then keep doing that for your whole life. God only knows what will happen." Not exactly something you'd put on a T-shirt, is it?[56]

We're resistant to this kind of thing because it's too vague—and the specific alternatives are so much easier. Writing a check instead of entering a relationship with someone who might challenge our faith? Yes please! And never mind *sustaining* that relationship once the novelty has worn off. So we go on a missions trip once a year. Or buy a book about a "cause" for someone. Or we blog.

I've done all of those things. I get it. But these simply aren't the primary responses we're invited to make as followers of Jesus. Remember, it always comes down to loving God and loving our neighbor.

The thing about loving God is that it's unpredictable. And loving our neighbor? Uncomfortable.

I'm preaching to myself here. But it's vital that we get this stuff right. As our world becomes increasingly globalized *and* increasingly tribal and insular, we need to prioritize and fight for relationships. Relationships reveal need and provide opportunity, and it is through relationships—with the resources of God's Spirit—that we build holy, redemptive, kingdom communities.

Again, what does that actually *look* like?

---

[56] Trademark pending ... let me know if you want to be the first to buy a T-shirt.

It looks like equipping indigenous leaders to address the areas of greatest need in their communities.

It looks like intentionally seeing the world through the experiences and wisdom of people who are different from you.

It looks like having friends—both locally and globally—that surprise your cultural peers.

It looks like asking questions, even if you suspect you won't like the answer.

It can look like saying or doing things that make your church and your friends uncomfortable.

It can look like making your family uncomfortable.

It can look like making your accountant or your board uncomfortable.

We've got to dig deep for this stuff. If we're not willing to be wrong, we probably won't get it right.

But since when does a little hard work scare us? Since when do we not invest our heart, soul, mind, and strength when we know the return will be great?

A Broken Smile

All of these tensions and thoughts were tumbling around inside me the first time I met Mai.[57] I doubt if she remembers me, but I'll never forget her.

The SOLD Resource Center outside of Chiang Rai was teeming with happy, friendly kids, but Mai stood out. She shone brighter somehow. A high-energy rascal, she was quick to smile or frown, always vivacious. That initial attachment is probably why the twists and turns of her unfolding story hit me so hard. She was just a *kid* still, which is why it was so jarring to learn her biography. She gave a personality

---

[57] Not her real name. Some of this material is adapted from rachelgoble.com.

to the sometimes overwhelming, faceless problem of exploitation and trafficking.[58]

It's easy, in hindsight, to see how Mai's life went off course back when she was fifteen.

She missed her dad, but he was working in Bangkok and probably wasn't coming back. Her mom, while affectionate, was on the losing end of decades of drug and alcohol abuse. Mom had been exploited as a child, worked as a prostitute, and never got past second grade in school. Perhaps it's understandable that she would have a child with a man mostly unfit to be a father and that she would seek to numb her memories of a life that had always been painful.

And there was Mai herself, as curious, restless, and unable to think about the future as anyone her age. What was the world outside her village like? She didn't know, but whatever it was like, it had to be better than the constant boredom she endured. There was only one way to find out.

It started online. Mai didn't have a cell phone—until an older woman befriended Mai and offered to give her one. All she'd need to do in return was listen to a few things the woman had to say. Like how there was so much more to life than Mai knew. Like how she could get as much as $1,000 for her virginity.

That cell phone allowed Mai to use Facebook and to connect with a certain boy the woman had told her about. On Facebook, there were always new faces and new places to imagine, but she connected most often with the boy. He seemed to understand what no one else did: that she was made for more than her boring little village, and that she was a woman.

---

[58] You may have heard people, after they visit some other country, say things like, "I just wish I could have taken that child home with me." You won't be surprised to know that elicits less-than-gentle thoughts from me. Except now I understand where that instinct comes from. I felt something grandfatherly toward Mai. But even though I have empathy for that instinct, it's still the wrong move most of the time. Ripping a child out of her context isn't the answer ... changing her context is.

They began dating, and he gained her trust. He convinced her to go to a karaoke bar in a business district about an hour away from her home.

That might have been the first chapter in a horror story that happens every single day in Thailand, as well as in countless countries across the world.

Except Mai had people who cared about her. They followed her digital trail and located her at the karaoke bar. When they arrived, they discovered Mai dancing atop a table in a provocative outfit, her youthful face hidden behind heavy makeup. They were able to get her to walk out with them before anything happened, because of course it wasn't just a karaoke bar.

They dared to walk into that dark place and take Mai with them, back to a safe house in Chiang Rai, and the next day back to her mother.

Then, a few days later, Mai disappeared in the middle of the night. The staff didn't find her for three days. And when they did, they discovered she'd been drugged and raped by her so-called boyfriend.

Some of the details will never be known. Was her disappearance an example of thwarted trafficking, or simply manipulation and coercion? Did anything else happen to her? Whatever the full story is, none of it should have happened to Mai. It should never happen to any child, yet it does—with disturbing regularity.

I wish I had something more profound to say, but Mai's story broke my heart. The only thing that made it bearable was knowing she was surrounded by smart, faithful, patient people who were committed to loving her and helping to keep her safe.

Not enough kids in Mai's position have that. How do we help them?

Sometimes with a donation from our couch. Sometimes by moving to Thailand. Sometimes we avoid the fact that kids like Mai are also trafficked in *our* cities. And sometimes we simply forget.

The Exchange of Hope

What needs to happen for someone like Mai to recover? What does life look like on the other side of a trauma like that?

Everyone is unique, of course, but I believe that healing goes hand in hand with hope. Hope is what gives us the energy, the vision, to keep living when life feels unlivable. A life stripped of hope is like a black hole. Hopeless people cannot dream, cannot think beyond the pain of the moment. Hopelessness tells us the lie that the past determines the future.

The presence of hope, however, changes everything. I'm not just talking about hopeful *words,* though. The book of James is a gut-punch on this issue.

Dear friends, do you think you'll get anywhere in this if you learn all the right words but never do anything? Does merely talking about faith indicate that a person really has it? For instance, you come upon an old friend dressed in rags and half-starved and say, "Good morning, friend! Be clothed in Christ! Be filled with the Holy Spirit!" and walk off without providing so much as a coat or a cup of soup—where does that get you? Isn't it obvious that God-talk without God-acts is outrageous nonsense? (James 2:14–17, MSG)

Our souls don't flourish on the mere *promise* of hope. When it comes to actually *living,* people need more than nice words. They need actual hope, hope that "does not disappoint."

When I consider the source of such hope in my own life, I imme-diately think of my relationship with D'Aun. I see the world through different lenses because of our relationship. It's both inevitable and beneficial that I ask myself, "What will D'Aun think about this?" or "I can't wait to share this with D'Aun." Loving D'Aun, and being loved by her, is a source of real hope. We *act* for each other as best as we are able.

This isn't unique to marriage. I believe the natural outcome of any kingdom relationship is hope.

The poor and I can teach each other.

The poor and I can pray for each other.

We can laugh and cry and process and celebrate and invent and mourn and advocate and bank and travel and rescue and sing and legislate and obey and endure. Together. Like an olive tree naturally bears olives, holy relationships naturally produce hope. The Christ-centered exchange of hope, anchored in relationship and empowered by God's Spirit.

* * *

I experienced this Christ-centered exchange of hope in a hut in Myanmar.

Myanmar sits at the intersection of millennia. A team of oxen pulls a rickety wagon past a parked Lamborghini. Signs for Coke and Marlboro compete for attention with the carved arch of an ancient Buddhist pagoda. Traditional rice farmers sell their harvest in markets stalls beside pirated DVDs.

I was there at the invitation of Jonathan, a Burmese national.[59] He leads a loose network of house churches in the region of Thaton, a part of the world (like Chiang Rai) that will doubtless see massive change in the years ahead. Jonathan also oversees a children's home and a job-creation program, and he preaches several times a week. I met a few other Americans who support Jonathan in Rangoon, where we hopped in a van and drove the 250 kilometers to an unnamed gathering of huts.

"Now I'm going to take you," he told us in broken English, "to church."

In the distance I could see a handful of dim lights from the rest of the village. But houses were few and far between so far out in the countryside, and the surrounding land alternated between hand-tilled fields and patches of dense forest.

Jonathan led us into the trees, and every trace of light disappeared. The only other place I'd been in such pure blackness was in the middle of the rainforest in Belize. Countless times there, whether coming back from a neighboring village or simply taking a walk before bed, I'd clicked off my headlights or flashlight and let the darkness

---

[59] Not his real name. And if you're confused by the Myanmar/Burma debate, so is everyone else.

flood over me. It's something we're simply not used to in developed countries. But we still had to follow Jonathan, so using our phones as flashlights, we made our way through the tightly packed bamboo.

Before long we came to a clearing where four small houses were clumped together. Each house was square, roughly fifteen or twenty feet to a side, and rose above the ground on bamboo stilts. When I reached the top of the ladder, I discovered the room was already full—a few dozen people, who were smiling at me in welcome.

I stepped tentatively across the room, only to punch my foot right through the floor.[60] Eventually I managed to retreat to a safe place against one of the walls, where I sat cross-legged like everyone else.

There were three, maybe four generations gathered. The oldest was the patriarch of the farming community. I estimated his age at fifty or sixty, though I could have been way off. He and his family had lost everything in the 2011 tsunami and moved north to start over.

Everyone in the room—as far as I could tell, of course—was deeply in love with Jesus.

As I ate the sliced fruit and simple candies offered to me, I was struck by the enormous contrasts here. The differences between myself and the gathered worshippers were so numerous, so significant, that even to list them seems absurd. We lived on the same planet, but we didn't remotely live the same lives.

And yet.

Through the translator, I heard familiar words of faith. I hummed along with voices raised in praise. I sensed God's Spirit.

In short, I understood that they were hungry for the same thing I was: hope.

The contrasts in our world are sharp enough to cut, but there are two similarities between every place on earth that, I'm convinced, are more important than any differences. Those two similarities are change and hunger for hope. Every place on earth is changing, and

---

[60] I realize I was the largest person in a 200 kilometer radius. But it was still embarrassing.

everyone on earth is hungry for hope. Hope for a way out. Hope for a job. Hope for a child. Hope for meaning or purpose.

When I left Myanmar, I ended up in a flophouse near the Bangkok airport, sharing my rickety bed with what seemed like a thousand starving fleas.

And I was filled with hope.

Not because of me, but because of the people God has placed in my life. Because of holy kingdom relationships with people unimaginably different than me. And because I knew that the Christ-centered exchange of hope is what builds the kingdom and changes our world.

Free to Fail

I never told you the end of Mai's story.

When she was rescued from the karaoke bar, she was taken to the resource center in Chiang Rai. She'd been given a second chance. She'd been saved. Which is why you might be surprised to learn the rest of her story.

Freedom is one of those words that doesn't mean much apart from the context of a life. Freedom *from* what? Freedom *for* what? The folks at the resource center had an agonizing set of decisions to make about Mai's freedom. They'd set her free from a life of sexual abuse … which meant she was free to make her own choices.

The hope was that she'd focus on her studies. Perhaps she'd attend university. Perhaps she'd use the resources she'd been given in order to help the next generation of girls growing up just like she had.

Instead, at seventeen she married a local boy. She got pregnant. And just like that, the track of her life became almost impossible to change. No more school, many fewer choices. If she lived in my town, she'd be partway through high school. In her village, she was already a housewife.

I wish I had a conclusion to offer you. Some kind of neat ending that would tie up all the loose ends. The best narrative is the black-and-white one, where an innocent girl is rescued from an evil trafficker. End scene.

But this is a story that goes beyond that kind of simple distinction. The fact that something is wrong doesn't make the right answer obvious. At a minimum we need to remind ourselves that Mai is a living, breathing, changing person. She is free to make choices. She is free to fail. Those who exploited her are people too. God loves them, which won't bother most of us. But God commands *us* to love them too, and that's a hell of a lot harder to accept.

Beyond that, we need to remind ourselves that lives aren't snapshots. They're ongoing stories. Mai's story isn't finished yet. No one's story is finished yet. Our world, our culture, is all about the moment. Instant everything. In the kingdom, though, there's the end, and there's the *end*. Only God knows that ultimate end, just like God is the only one who can love the whole freaking world—including me, including Mai, including every person who decides to abuse a child.

And God isn't done working.

When we provide freedom to someone who has been enslaved, that's exactly what we're doing—providing freedom. Freedom to study, to dream, to make decisions, to live a new life—but flip that same coin, and you get freedom to fail, to hurt yourself and others, to go back into slavery. The reality is that each of us is helpless to truly control other people. It won't work with fear. It won't even work with love.

What's a follower of Jesus to do with stories like Mai's?

What am *I* supposed to do with this story?

I could fly to Thailand and provide Mai and her husband with everything they need to break the cycle of poverty and hopelessness that will almost certainly trap them: an education fund, health care, job training. But should I? If so, who else should I help in a similar way? If not, why? And how in the world does all of that relate to how I love my neighbor—across the street, across town—as God commands me to?

These are the questions I've been wrestling with for decades. And I expect them to continue, damn it. God help me, but I really do wish he'd just make it all clear.

Sometimes difficult issues can't be solved from a distance, but they can't be solved from up close either. This world we call home is complicated. Achingly, sinfully, frustratingly complicated. Yet it's the very world in which God has placed us and commanded us to love.

God loves the world. God's the only one who *can* love the world. And part of God's plan for loving the world involves us. God asks those who would follow him to do two things: to love God and to love our neighbor with our whole being.

Yet we miss that mark constantly. Does Jesus slap his forehead in frustration? *I gave you* two *simple things to do.*

Even then we'd be full of blustering protest. *But I've been a Christian my whole life. But I tithe. But I said the sinner's prayer and put my trust in Jesus.*

But, but, but ...

Love is doing real things for real people. It results in holy relationships. It builds the kingdom. Our command to love God and love others is *the* command. It's literally the only thing we need to worry about. Jesus is quite specific about that.

So how can such a simple command be so hard to understand and live?

At the end of the day, loving God and loving others is the only answer we can have to the questions that plague us. And that is the farthest thing from sentimental sappiness. In fact, loving others is the hardest, most uncertain, most unpredictable thing we will ever do. It is so difficult that we cannot do it without help. We need the help of others we meet along the way. We need friends who are creative, and entrepreneurial, and patient, and righteously angry, and from a different culture, and brave.

And we need the help of God. Every day, every place. Through his Spirit, God wants us to bear fruit for the sake of this broken world—and for the sake of our own broken lives. If we don't remain in Christ, there can be no fruit. We simply can't do it by ourselves.

Maybe that's what God had in mind when he commanded us to do the impossible.

Maybe that's why we follow Jesus instead of a set of rules.

Maybe that's why we've got to keep wrestling.

~9~

CONCLUSION

Back in the 1950s, my parents owned a small house in town, and for a few years they rented it to a young couple. At one point, the couple fell several months behind on their rent, so Dad asked Mom to drive over and find out why. A harried-looking young woman holding a crying baby answered Mom's knock. When Mom explained the reason for her visit, the woman began to cry. They had no money, she confessed, even though her husband was looking for work, all day every day. She pleaded for a bit more time to scrape the rent together, then blurted out, "I don't even have money to take my baby to the doctor, and she's burning up!"

Mom reached forward, only to flinch when she touched the girl's hot forehead. The baby should have been taken to the hospital hours, if not days, earlier. Mom started to ask if they'd seen a doctor, only to be interrupted again by the mother, in a small, sheepish voice, "But I don't even have a car!"

Mom immediately bundled the unhappy woman and her screaming baby into the back of whichever rebuilt junkyard car she was driving at the time, and the three of them raced to the hospital. Paperwork was followed by an unpleasant wait, but at last they were ushered into the doctor's office. The baby would probably be fine, they were soon told, but just barely—any more delay and there would have been a tragic ending.

Mom paid the hospital bill on the way out the door, naturally.

Later that day, when Mom was back home, Dad asked about the rent check. Mom answered with a description of the sweet young

123

family, along with a blow-by-blow account of saving the baby's life. "I was able to give that poor young lady a few parenting tips too," Mom concluded, a sense of awe and accomplishment in her voice.

Dad couldn't believe it: he'd sent her to *collect* rent, and instead she'd ended up spending money! That was the last time Dad ever sent Mom to collect rent from one of their tenants.

In so many ways I'm the son of my parents.

I want to collect rent and to help people in need. I want to create wealth to give it away. I never want to be taken advantage of, and I always want to be available to listen and help.

When I was a boy running loose in Dad's junkyard, my current life would have been unimaginable. Yet much of who I am—how I think, where I've been, the way I act—is a direct consequence of spending my formative years in close contact with the rough-and-tumble characters at my dad's business. If not for the junkyard, would I have shut down emotionally during my first visit to the Klong Toey slum—or stayed away entirely? Is there a chance I would have never dreamed about Belize or partnered with Old Skool Cafe? Might Mai have remained nothing more than a statistic?

One downside of the junkyard mentality, though, is that it doesn't care much about the complicated solutions to complex problems. In the junkyard, things tend to be simple. You see a car and you pull it apart. You see a customer and you swap a part for a payment. If an employee isn't working out, you fire him. In that world there just isn't a lot of time—or even need—for nuance or reflection.

So what's a Jesus-following junkyard kid supposed to do with things like generational poverty and child trafficking? Or environmental degradation, lack of educational opportunities, racism, exploitation, homelessness, and hunger? These things are exceedingly tough to tackle.

There's the problem: those things aren't *things*.

We're not talking about "conditions of our world" or "regrettable consequences of political corruption." We're talking about *people*. Men, women, and children, created in God's image, loved by their Creator, and infinitely valuable. I can't comprehend their pain, let alone fix it.

All I know is that I must keep my eyes open.

* * *

Except paying attention is a *choice*, because disappearing into the fog of luxury is an ever-present option for me. Whenever I choose, I can envelop myself in comfort. I can return to the Raffles Hotel in Singapore and thoroughly insulate myself.

Wealth is a master illusionist.

My money, and the privilege that goes along with it, can make it *seem* as if everything revolves around *me*—and as if everyone else is actually pleased with that arrangement. Like when the Raffles staff laugh at any joke I make, no matter how stupid, and when they insist it's their pleasure to change my dinner reservation for the third time.

In Singapore, I've seen women wrapped in $10,000 dresses and men wrapped in $200,000 sports cars. I've seen a woman on a trapeze soar to select a bottle of wine thirty feet above the restaurant floor. I've luxuriated in a hotel room larger than any home in Klong Toey. I've savored coffee so expensive it could provide a week's worth of food for a family in Cite Soleil. I've been shuttled from the hotel to the airport in a car so pricey it could fund enough microenterprise ventures to employ thousands.

In Hong Kong I've seen shoes so expensive their price would clothe a poor family for life.

In London I've been served high tea for two that costs more than half a billion people make in a year.

In Silicon Valley I've seen millionaires making more money for billionaires.

Wealth can be an extremely pleasant way to suffocate. And it isn't just me. Many of us in the West are suffocating in comfort and wealth and privilege and distraction. And it can be so pleasant that we almost don't hear that little voice whispering to us.[61]

---

[61] Plus, sometimes we have our fingers shoved in our ears.

"Whatever you did for one of the least of these brothers and sisters of mine, you did for me."[62]

"'Love the Lord your God with all your heart and with all your soul and with all your mind.' This is the first and greatest commandment. And the second is like it: 'Love your neighbor as yourself.' All the Law and the Prophets hang on these two commandments."[63]

Aren't we sometimes *happy* to believe the illusions of wealth?

Any wealth inevitably separates us from those who are less wealthy, and that can start to seem normal. Day to day, our interactions tend to be with three kinds of people: others who are like us, others who are wealthier than us, and those whose job it is to serve us. Practically speaking, the poor don't exist in the world of wealth, unless of course they have been given strict orders to smile as they serve.

Exploitation may be the farthest thing from our minds. We don't tend to actively disparage or abuse the poor. We don't sit around the dinner table or at church or in the boardroom and laugh at those who have less. It's simply that when we are surrounded by people so similar to us, *we forget the poor.*

We forget Mai. We forget the man in Haiti wearing a tragicomic T-shirt. We forget the neighborhood we avoid driving through on the way to work.

So I have to ask myself the hard questions, over and over.

Which world am I living in?

Am I creating a world for myself—even if it's unintentional—where I never see the poor?

Am I paying attention?

Those weren't tensions that preoccupied me when I was stacking old tires in the junkyard. Now, though, they represent the kind of wrestling that God asks me to do. In fact, I think it's the kind of wrestling I was *designed* to do. Because God knew I wouldn't be in that junkyard forever—just like God knew I wouldn't be able to forget it.

---

[62] Matt 25:40
[63] Matt 22:37–40

What the Poor Deserve

I am a member of Christ's body, the universal church. That sounds nice! It's the kind of truth that can give you warm fuzzies, spiritually speaking.

Here's another truth: I am a wealth creator.

Hmm. That's not *quite* as appealing for some reason. But I *am* a wealth creator, just like I'm a member of Christ's body.

And believe me, that tension can cause problems.

Once on a trip to Belize, I brought along an intern from our US staff. We had a group of college kids staying on the property already, studying tropical biology and sustainable development. I wanted to lead a conversation over dinner that would help us confront some of the deep issues affecting our world and our hearts. So after a prayer of thanks, I looked around the table and, hoping to stimulate some conversation, I asked the simple question, "If you won a million dollars, what would you do with it?"

Right away the intern piped up with, "I'd give it all away. Money is evil ... and anyone with a lot of money is suspect."

Present company *not* excluded! The organization I'd developed and grown paid his salary. He'd flown to Belize on my dime, where he was being hosted at a complex I built. Oh, and he was chatting with students who were part of a program I created and funded. Monetary donations, most of which came from individuals who had a lot of money by global standards, allowed us to serve the poor around the world and protect God's creation.

And yet, knowing all of that, the intern would take a million dollars and "give it all away." Not invest it. Not grow it. Not pray about how to best utilize it to fulfill the Great Commission and the Great Commandment. Why? Because he viewed money as evil—and if he kept it, he'd be tainted as well.[64]

---

[64] Maybe I shouldn't have flown him back to the States—first class, of course—with my frequent flyer miles!

I wish his comment were thoughtless and uncommon.

Unfortunately it is neither. In communities of all kinds, all around the world, I've encountered a knee-jerk opposition to money and wealth creation. Even in the church, far too many thoughtful, prayerful, well-meaning Christians believe a variation of that opinion. Even though Jesus clearly tells us that *loving* money is the root of evil, rather than money itself, some of us take a better-safe-than-sorry approach and simply condemn cash. By extension, the people *with* the cash get condemned as well. By my staffer's logic, everyone with "extra" money should give it away, to avoid being contaminated.

Does the *potential* for evil hide within money? Yes—but so does the potential for great good. That same potential for goodness hides inside many human creations, like art and education. The fact that art can become propaganda, or that education can become indoctrination, doesn't deter most Christians from valuing art and education.

Too often we label money, uniquely, as the one fallen human creation that's beyond redemption. This is deeply ironic, considering how gung-ho many Christians are about the redemption of everything else! We acknowledge that everything is fallen and that everything fallen needs to be redeemed, yet we exclude money as irredeemably flawed and evil. Hence comments like the one from the intern.

My role as a wealth creator is *one* part I play in the functioning of Christ's body. But just like it doesn't describe the totality of who I am and who Christ calls me to be, neither should I ignore it. And neither should the church ignore it! If I thought my ability to create wealth made me special, I'd be wrong, but I'd also be wrong not to utilize that ability for God's kingdom.

We stuff other people into boxes, almost like a reflex: villain, celebrity, saint, sinner. But sometimes, following Jesus means subjugating *our* reflexes in favor of *God's*.[65]

---

[65] Like when Jesus tells us not to resist an evil person who's attacking us, but instead to "turn the other cheek." That goes against *every* human reflex—and yet Jesus commands his followers to do it anyway.

The tough part is, our reflexes can be wrong, even when they seem motivated by all the right reasons. Here's an example.

College Kid: I've got all this privilege, and I'm living in this on-campus bubble, and I know that the world is filled with so much tragedy … so shouldn't I be doing something real that makes a difference, instead of selfishly studying in comfort?[66]

Me: Are you freaking *kidding* me?!?

I've had quite a few variations on conversations like that one. Sometimes instead of a college kid, it's a young tech entrepreneur wanting to quit his position or a financial advisor worried about the morality of her job. Whenever this kind of question has come up, I've wanted to shout, "You've got stock options that could build a thousand classrooms in India, and you want to give that up so you can hand out sandwiches on the street? Don't be an idiot!"

(Full disclosure: I *have* shouted this, once. Usually I manage to just think it.)

Lately, however, I've been shown a better way. A wiser, more measured response to a question—a longing, really—that comes from an admirable place. We want to follow Jesus, and we want to make a difference, and we want to be good neighbors to our fellow humans and good stewards of the environment. Those are godly impulses.

It's just that they don't necessarily lead directly to becoming the next Saint Francis.

So when I have these conversations now, I try to ask that person if they have begun to love the world—in the sense the apostle John warns us about.

This sounds like a paradox. But when we fall in love with the world, we insulate ourselves *from* the world. And if we are still trying to follow Jesus, that insulated life will make us guilty. What's the best way to relieve our guilt at that point? Passing out sandwiches can feel like a good start … and then it's back to our insulated life.

---

[66] Kids are still articulate these days. Don't let anyone tell you otherwise.

Next, I try to remind that person that the poor deserve our *best*.

Because we think helping the poor is easy, we think helping the poor doesn't require our best. It only takes a weekend. Or a bit of money. Or some emails and tweets. Or a recurring deposit. So often we help the poor, if we help them at all, with laziness and platitudes and activities designed more to salve our consciences than to provide real hope.

From this point on, I propose that no one is allowed to say "I want to help the poor" unless that person is willing to give their very best. That might mean staying in college until you've earned a master's degree in cross-cultural studies or until you can perform eye surgeries. It might mean getting your contractor's license or a degree in microfinance or one of the ten thousand other valuable skills needed to actually *help* the poor and not simply wish them well or give them a token of our good intentions.

I know students and professionals will continue to ask, "Shouldn't I be doing something real that makes a difference?"

Wanting to make a difference is great! But the correct answer is, "What makes you think you aren't *already* doing something real that will make a difference?"

When we wealthy cheat ourselves, we cheat the poor.

You know when passing out sandwiches is a good thing? When we see Christ in the people we're serving and they see Christ in us. As Saint Patrick's famous prayer puts it,

Be in the heart of each to whom I speak
Be in the mouth of each who speaks to me

Being part of Christ's body isn't about checklists, even when you're a wealth creator. Following Jesus is about relationships.

If you're anything like me, you could always use more relationships with people who are different than you.

And if you're anything like me, you could always work harder to give everyone you meet—friends, neighbors, strangers, and especially the poor—your absolute best.

Living Close to Hell

Our prejudices are partly right. Depravity *does* live in the soul of money ... but so does sainthood.

In that sense, money is not different from the human heart. We are continually conflicted creatures. In the bloodiest century of human history, a Christian who was persecuted and tortured wrote this:

If only there were evil people somewhere insidiously committing evil deeds, and it were necessary only to separate them from the rest of us and destroy them. But the line dividing good and evil cuts through the heart of every human being. And who is willing to destroy a piece of his own heart?[67]

It would be simpler to view money in purely black-and-white terms, but that does not match reality. Wealth has shaped me in ways that nobody, least of all me, can ever fully understand. Sometimes wealth has been a blessing, other times a curse.

How am I, a man who desires to follow Christ and become more like him, to respond to such a tension?

In his book *Freedom of Simplicity*, Richard Foster writes this:

Wealth is not for the spiritual neophytes; they will be destroyed by it... This path is fraught with great frustrations and temptations, and those who walk it have to face perplexing decisions and tragic moral choices that most people will never have to consider ... We [the wealthy] will be living close to hell for the sake of heaven.[68]

That final phrase fascinates me. If the potential for depravity lives in the soul of money, it follows that a correlation exists between the amount of money one has and the proximity to hell—to idolatry, exploitation, and pride. But if Foster is correct, there can be a redeeming purpose in that proximity. If we wealthy understand *where* they are living, perhaps we can embrace the *why*: for the sake of heaven.

---

[67] Solzhenitsyn, who understood the potential of money for both good and evil.
[68] *Freedom of Simplicity*, page 53.

A Hut and a Tux

When a wealthy person's desire for God (and for loving others) is replaced by a desire for money or status or power, the battle has already been lost. So how do we guard against that happening?

One of the best defenses is realizing that the battle is happening in the first place, along with the fact that *we* are the ones living close to the gates of hell.

Contained in that is good news. Wealth creation can be a powerful weapon for God's kingdom. A rich person living at the gates of hell is in a dangerous spot—but if that person is following Jesus, they *become* dangerous. Dangerous to evil. Dangerous to hopelessness and injustice. The wealthy constantly shape and influence the world, whether consciously or not. Imagine what would happen if that influence was guided by the example of Jesus and empowered by the Spirit!

Spurgeon once expressed a wish in line with this reality: to live where he couldn't hear church bells. He meant living where the gospel had not yet been established, far from the comfort of his Christian community. Perhaps today we would express that differently. *Living on the bleeding edge of kingdom building*—how does that sound?

Whatever we call it, it's what we want to be doing with our lives. It's what *you* want, or you wouldn't be reading still. We want to use our wealth—including our cultural influence and education and skills—to make this world better. God loves the world, but we can't. We can only love the people we come into contact with, and the only way to love people who are different than ourselves is to be intentional about it. To change the way we shop and drive and vacation and work and spend.

If we're going to do this, we're going to need allies. None of us can pull this off alone. More importantly, we can't do this if we only know people who are exactly the same as us. Finding partners we can learn from and work with, to one extent or another, is vital.

Consider the following "opposites" which, if we're honest, we must admit are actually spectrums:

Rich and poor
West and east
North and south
Developed and developing
Liberal and conservative
Educated and uneducated
Foolish and wise
Old and young
Christian and other religion
Christian and atheist
Married and widowed and divorced and single
Sick and healthy
Straight and gay and anything else
Extroverted and introverted
Daring and risk averse
Creative and businesslike

Think of a traditional graph with X and Y axes. We can plot and describe a great deal of information on a graph with only two directions. Now imagine a graph with nearly *infinite* axes. With all the contrasts I just mentioned, along with a whole lot more. Only God could understand something so complicated, so full of possibility— and that's the God who dreamed up ways for us to build the kingdom before we were even born. The poor need the rich, the rich need the poor, and *all* of us can live the Great Commission.

If we're going to change the world, we need allies who are different than we are. We need every possible weapon: every business plan and prayer and cultural insight and language and income level. These become the tools God uses to break down the walls between his children.

We're going to need more than collaboration, though, if we're going to fight at the gates of hell: we're also going to need courage. Or at least a willingness to look foolish, because a lot of what we do will freak people out. Every institution in our culture—including, unfortunately, the church—tends to reinforce and maintain social conventions.

There's an interesting example of this in Isaiah 57. Beginning in verse 15, the author warns us that something deep is coming: *"For this is what the high and exalted One says—he who lives forever, whose name is holy."* I'm pretty sure it's important to pay attention after that introduction. Then come the very words of God.

I live in a high and holy place,
but also with the one who is contrite and lowly in spirit,
to revive the spirit of the lowly
and to revive the heart of the contrite.

God isn't sequestered far away in heaven, unaware of what's happening down on this tiny, flawed chunk of interstellar rock. God understands the high places and the low places, and he loves them both.

And God wants the same for us.

We are in a unique position to live in a high place *and* a contrite place—to enter into relationships with the powerful and the vulnerable. When we do, we can become translators in both directions. The poor cannot typically decide to begin friendships with the wealthy. They don't have the access.

The wealthy do. We are the ones who must choose to tear down those walls—as much (or more) for our sake as the sake of the poor.

My aim as a wealthy follower of Jesus is to be as comfortable in a mud hut as I am in a tux at a formal event ... and to continue making myself present at both! I'm still uncomfortable in both these roles, to be honest. But like any skill, the only way to get better is to practice.

Where will you begin your journey between a hut and a tux? And what stories of hope will you translate between the two?

This isn't a philosophy book. I'm not an academic. My heart isn't to convince you of anything, but rather to invite you to make a stand where you are—at the gates of hell—and fight for the sake of heaven. I believe you'll accept that invitation. Partly because you know you have an incredible amount to offer a hurting world. And partly because you want to hear, today as well as in eternity, the words, "Well done, good and faithful servant."

Chrysostom's Question

"So what is the skill that rich people should acquire?"

That's the question asked by Saint John Chrysostom, Archbishop of Constantinople, over a thousand years ago.[69] It's thorny because it has so many possible answers. It's the kind of question we're afraid to answer because we'll probably get it wrong. That is why it's easier to ignore it ... or even to reject the premise. Rather than answering, we can shut down the conversation.

For example, if we simply tell rich people to give away all their money, then no skill is required.

Let me share more of Chrysostom's thought, though, because he offers some compelling evidence that living as a rich Christian does, in fact, require significant *skill*. He continues:

They must learn how to use their wealth well, to the good of all the people around them. The ordinary craftsperson may think that that is an easy skill to learn. On the contrary, it is the hardest skill of all. It requires both great wisdom and great moral strength. Look at how many rich people fail to acquire it, and how few practice it to perfection.

To this point, Chrysostom is advocating something everyone agrees to: the rich should use their wealth for the greater good rather than selfish indulgence. Our culture admires billionaires because they're billionaires, but we tend to like the ones who try to cure cancer better than the ones who buy four sports franchises and a private

---

[69] His slogan should be: "Provoking believers since the 4th century CE."

submarine. *But if using wealth well was easy,* he basically says, *we wouldn't be surrounded by quite so many rich ...* never mind—my junkyard language almost slipped out.

We haven't reached the most provocative portion of Chrysostom's insight, however. What follows is long, but read all of it.

The skill which the rich need to use their wealth well is the highest of all arts. Its workshop is built not on earth but in heaven, because those who are rich must communicate directly with God to acquire and practice this art. Its tools are not made of iron or brass, but of good will, because the rich will only use their wealth well if they want to do so. Indeed good will is itself the skill. When a rich person sincerely wants to help the poor, God will quickly show the best way. Thus while a person training to be a carpenter must learn how to control a hammer and saw and chisel, the rich person training to serve the poor must learn how to control the mind and heart and soul. He must learn always to think good thoughts, expunging all selfish thoughts. He must learn how to feel compassion, expunging all malice and contempt. He must learn how to desire only to obey the will of God. That is why I say the skill of being a rich disciple of Christ is the highest of all arts; and the one who possesses it is truly a saint.[70]

Deep. And *so* difficult.

Following Jesus as a wealthy person is certainly a skill. To an extent, all of us need to learn that skill, because all of us are (in certain contexts) wealthy.

For some of us, however, this skill is of life-and-death importance. And unfortunately, skill in wealth creation has no correlation with skill in the godly use of wealth. We can be in the top tenth of 1 percent when it comes to the talent and acumen it takes to create wealth, yet remain absolute neophytes when it comes to being a "rich disciple of Christ."

Remember, a disciple is a *learner.* "When a rich person sincerely wants to help the poor," Chrysostom writes, "God will quickly show the best way."

---

[70] Thumbnail definition of "saint": an imperfect person willing and ready to be used by a perfect God.

That's how this stuff works: with a willingness to do the next thing. If you honestly ask God, right now, to show you a way to help the poor, an opportunity will present itself in the very near future. But then you have to seize that opportunity and act on it, even though you won't know where it leads.

When the Barkers left Australia to move to Klong Toey, they had no idea what would happen a month or a year down the road—they simply knew God would show them the best way, and they were willing to learn. Or think of Pastor Carol Houston traveling for the first time from downtown Los Angeles to the Belizean rainforest, or Teresa Goines taking the first steps toward building Old Skool Cafe from a vision into a reality.

Trust and obedience are the way this works. God doesn't give us a five-year or fifty-year plan we can sign off on. If we trust enough to obey *today*, God will show us what we need for tomorrow.

Too often, though, we trust our checkbooks and obey our desires. When we do, that sound we hear is the gates of hell swinging open.

"True ministry," writes Henri Nouwen, "goes far beyond the giving of gifts."

As with Chrysostom, that's only the start of a quote. The reason I interrupted it is so I could make sure *I* pay close attention to what's coming next. This is tough stuff. Part of me wants true ministry to start and stop with the giving of gifts. Even if I gave past what was comfortable, or gave sacrificially, it would be far easier than what Nouwen is about to say.

But I'm quoting him here because another part of me—and I can honestly say, by God's grace and patience, that it's now the bigger part of me—is ready to hear what "true ministry" requires.

It requires giving of self. That is the way of him who did not cling to his privileges but emptied himself to share our struggles. When God's way becomes known to us, and practiced by us, hope emerges.[71]

---

[71] Nouwen. *Gracias! A Latin American Journal* entry dated December 25th.

Hope is what we're chasing, all 7.3 billion of us. A Christ-centered exchange of hope happens when we give ourselves away. When we empty ourselves. Because when we do this for the sake of Christ, we will always be refilled.

The Feast of the Unfamiliar

This life I'm describing—using your wealth for the sake of heaven—is not the path between extremes. It's not the least or the lowest common denominator. It is not a "middle way" or a compromise between wealth and poverty. This isn't about splitting your time between relying on God and relying on money.

On the contrary, this is a new way. Not new because no one has ever tried it, but new because it is "new every morning." It is different for each of us. It is a thrilling and unexpected way. Living this way requires your faith to grow and your mind to stretch. It is provocative and exciting in all the right ways. Rather than the average of various ways to live, this can be the best of all possible worlds.

When we choose something, we exclude something else. In choosing safety we hope to exclude risk. We choose comfort because we prefer it to discomfort. Yet Scripture guarantees three things in life.

We will have trouble in this world.

Christ has overcome this world.

There is a world beyond this world.[72]

So take heart! The control we supposedly exert over our lives is an illusion. It is the good gifts of God that are the real stuff of life. The new relationships. The changed lives. The rescues and redemptions. And yes, even the difficult times. Even the illnesses and deaths and firings and fights. Even these can be part of a life that is a *feast of the unfamiliar.*[73]

---

[72] John 14–17

[73] Credit to my friend Keaton Hudson for this phrase. I'll tell you the story behind it if you ask me in person.

That's exactly what I love about it. Like a table covered in sumptuous, homemade food, I simply don't know what to savor first. There are endless variations of flavor and texture. And like any real meal, it's meant to be *shared*. It's meant to give us reasons to come together and celebrate for years to come.

I've talked a lot about the metaphor of wrestling, and it occurs to me that I might need to redefine how I'm using it. Wrestling can sound like never-ending work. Who wants to sign up for a lifetime of getting punched and pummeled?

When we were kids, though, we wrestled because it was *fun*. There's a pleasure in the contest, in the unknown outcome, in the give-and-take of the unexpected. If we believe God's promises, the unplanned isn't something to fear, but rather to explore and embrace. The spiritual pursuit can feel exhausting, yes—but that isn't the entire description. We must not miss the pure, flat-out *fun* of following Jesus.

Far too often we settle for a vision of life that comes from bad commencement speeches. "Embrace your passion and pursue your dreams!"

Um, no. All too often our passions are disordered and our dreams are only for ourselves—and they can be such petty, pathetic dreams! As Lewis mused,

It would seem that Our Lord finds our desires not too strong, but too weak. We are half-hearted creatures, fooling about with drink and sex and ambition when infinite joy is offered us, like an ignorant child who wants to go on making mud pies in a slum because he cannot imagine what is meant by the offer of a holiday at the sea. We are far too easily pleased.[74]

I'll confess that I have been far too easily pleased in my life, but now I *know* that God has something better waiting for me. I know that every time I look up from a mud pie, God shows me the sea.

---

[74] C.S. Lewis, *The Weight of Glory, and Other Addresses*

Life is about *God's* passion and the dreams of *others*. Chasing those is when we experience true joy and how we bring back stories to set on the table for others to savor.

This life God has shown me—the life of a wealthy Westerner following Jesus and remembering the poor—is the greatest adventure. It's powerfully intoxicating. I have a front-row seat to changed lives and changed communities. Changed hearts, including my own. I choose not to love the world, may God forgive my failures, and I choose to love the people in God's world.

In many ways I'm still that junkyard kid, familiar with the wrecked and rusty side of life. In other ways I've left the junkyard behind forever, rising to a level of wealth and influence I never could have imagined. Which is why I feel the obligation to make myself present in the forgotten places of our world.

So that I do not forget.

Not because those people need me to be their savior, but because my Savior has convinced me that *I* need *them*.

Even now you could choose to forget about this stuff. You could close the book and move on with life. Just as I could choose not to fly to Thailand again, or to work in Belize, or to partner with people who are transforming my state and my community. Running toward forgetfulness is a continual temptation.

Yet memories of the allies I've met chase after me, as do memories of those who continue to live with little hope, or none.

I could banish them from the world I inhabit.

I cannot banish them from my heart.

ACKNOWLEDGMENTS

(of ways I messed up)

I'm sorry to D'Aun for sometimes being too focused on this book and not enough on you. Thanks for letting me go on these adventures and often joining me. As I said in the dedication, I'm so glad I married you.

I'm sorry to Rachel and Jedd for not being a better dad. I'm always off on my next adventure, sometimes at the expense of your own. I'm forever indebted to you for encouraging me to start thinking about this book.

I'm sorry to Mom for not always modeling love for others, like you taught me. I'm sorry to Dad for not always listening to your advice about business and people, like you taught me. I'm sorry to both for becoming a weird hybrid mix of your passions.

I'm sorry to my cowriter, David, for never giving you a straight answer when you asked really excellent questions. You were amazing to work with, and I look forward to the next project.

I'm sorry to my assistant, Anne, for always using "But" at the start of a sentence; never, ever, using, commas quite right; and asking her to read the same thing over and over.

I'm sorry to the folks at Goble Properties for not giving you more recognition in this book. You make amazing things happen.

I'm sorry to the folks at PathLight for not always having my heart open to the transformative power of hope, faith, and learning. You amaze me.

I'm sorry to all the folks at The SOLD Project for not always having my heart open to the anguish of trafficking and the power of prevention. Thank you for all you do.

I'm sorry to many friends. Mark and Adrienne, thanks for keeping my Belize stories rooted in reality, and sorry for "remembering big." Brenda and Derek, your ideas and prayers are all over this book, and I apologize for making a mess of them. Mike Yankoski, thanks for connecting me with some great people in the publishing industry. Greg Lundell, thanks for reading early drafts without laughing out loud. One-Eyed Rich, Crazy Eddie, and my brother Geoff, thanks for the amazing stories.

I'm sorry to Ash, Teresa, and Carol for not writing a book that measures up to the inspiring work of your lives.

I'm sorry to Richard Foster for not living up to the inspiration of his writings on simplicity and not fully grasping the wisdom he shared during our conversation at his home in the woods.

I'm sorry for often seeing things through the eyes of a white, Western man who is trained in business. I'm sorry for any flawed theology, contradictory statements, edgy language, or bad grammar. All entirely my fault.

I'm sorry to you, the reader, for not being able to answer all your questions. Since I'm still learning, the answers to many of life's complex questions are still to come. I'll let you know if I figure them out, and I hope you will do the same for me. Let's stay in touch. You can email me at roy@junkyardwisdom.com or follow along by subscribing to junkyardwisdombook.com. If you'd like to visit Belize with me someday, visit www.junkyardwisdombelize.com.

Most of all, I'm sorry this book can't fully express the things Jesus has taught me. I tried my best, but only a few of the pages even hint at the amazing opportunities we will find if we dare to resist the whisper of wealth, tear down the walls between us, and begin loving our neighbor as God calls us to.

Roy Goble
March 27, 2016
Northern California

Roy Goble grew up working in his father's junkyard, where he learned to take apart absolutely anything and to evaluate everything for the value of its parts. After studying economics and business at Westmont College and marrying his high school sweetheart, D'Aun, he joined his family's growing real estate business. As the business flourished, he experienced the complexity of creating wealth while following Jesus. He began to wrestle with what he knew about business and what Jesus was calling him to be and do, beginning a decades-long quest for a way to understand his place in God's kingdom and in a global society.

Today Roy runs a real estate investment company based in Silicon Valley, leads the ministry PathLight International, and serves on multiple boards—while still finding time to visit and learn from friends and ministry partners around the world. Following Jesus as a wealth creator has turned out to be harder and better than he ever imagined, and sometimes he misses the simplicity of selling parts in the junkyard. After thirty-five years of marriage, however, D'Aun tells him he already owns too many old cars.

D.R. Jacobsen believes "that the story of any one of us is in some measure the story of us all," a conviction that shapes his collaborative writing and editing—and a phrase of Frederick Buechner's that he's fond of stealing. He holds a BA in English from Westmont College, an MA in theology from Regent College, and an MFA in creative writing from Seattle Pacific University. As David Jacobsen, his essays have appeared in various journals and anthologies, and he is the author of *Rookie Dad: Thoughts on First-Time Fatherhood*. As a collaborative writer he is represented by Don Jacobson of DC Jacobson & Associates. He and his wife have lived in California, Austria, and British Columbia, and now they make their home with their two boys in central Oregon. When not thinking about words, he plays pickup soccer, roots for the Timbers, and writes compelling bios. You can connect with him at jacobsenwriting.com.